Irrepressible
HOPE

Devotions *to* Anchor Your Soul
and Buoy Your Spirit

Patsy Clairmont ✿ Barbara Johnson

Nicole Johnson ✿ Marilyn Meberg ✿ Luci Swindoll

Sheila Walsh ✿ Thelma Wells

TRACI MULLINS, *General Editor*

IRREPRESSIBLE HOPE

Published by W Publishing Group, a division of Thomas Nelson, Inc., P.O. Box 141000, Nashville, Tennessee 37214.

Unless otherwise noted, all Scripture quotations are taken from The Holy Bible, New International Version. Copyright © 1973, 1978, 1984, International Bible Society. Used by permission of Zondervan Bible Publishers.

Other Scripture quotations are from the following sources:

The Holy Bible, New Living Translation (NLT), copyright © 1996. Used by permission of Tyndale House Publishers, Inc., Wheaton, Illinois. All rights reserved.

The New American Standard Bible (NASB), copyright © 1960, 1977 by the Lockman Foundation. Used by permission.

The Message (MSG), copyright © 1993. Used by permission of NavPress Publishing Group.

Library of Congress Cataloging-in-Publication Data

Irrepressible hope : devotions to anchor your soul and buoy your spirit / by
    Patsy Clairmont . . . [et al.] ; Traci Mullins, general editor.
      p. cm.
    ISBN 0-8499-1804-9 (hc)
    ISBN 0-8499-9133-1 (mp)
    1. Christian women—Prayer-books and devotions—English. 2. Hope—
Religious aspects—Christianity I. Clairmont, Patsy. II. Mullins, Traci, 1960–
BV4844.I79 2003
234'.25—dc22   2003014598

Printed in the United States of America
03 04 05 06 07 QW 9 8 7 6 5 4 3 2 1

Contents

INTRODUCTION

The Cape of Good Hope

NICOLE JOHNSON

~

In 1487 the explorer Bartholomeu Dias set sail from Portugal to find a sea route to the riches of the East. He was forced ashore at the southernmost tip of Africa, and he named the place Cape of Storms, alluding to the tempest he had endured. He was not able to continue his journey, but he was so convinced that he had discovered the route he was looking for that he later changed the name to Cape of Good Hope.

This promontory lies at the maritime crossroads of the world. It is here that the East first met the West in treacherous stormy waters. With over twenty-six recorded shipwrecks, it wasn't a place where you really wanted to hang out. But it was a place you not only had to endure but had to navigate your way through if you wanted to find the wealth on the other side.

Every woman is an explorer in her own right, searching for meaning and purpose and a way that will make her life richer and fuller. And like maritime explorers of old, most of us have been forced ashore at key times on our journey. The waves, the weather, and the danger stand in the way of our planned route to riches. Regardless of the form the obstacle takes—illness, financial crisis, divorce, depression—much of what we have worked and hoped for threatens to be doomed on the rocks straight ahead.

Fortunately, this is precisely the place we find hope. No one finds hope until she feels hopeless. No one looks for more meaning in life until she fears that life has lost much of its meaning. And no one can fully see how the cape of storms actually becomes the cape of good hope until she's rounded the other side.

As we search for the rich life offered to us in Christ, it is our hope that this book will reveal a clear route. We all need help navigating the rough waters at the crossroads of our lives. Sheila, Thelma, Patsy, Luci, Barbara, Marilyn, and I pray that these devotionals will open a new route to the East, so to speak, by marking the way of trust and peace in the midst of life's raging storms. And that way is Jesus, who himself said, "I am the way" (John 14:6). He is the route we are looking for. His love and care are what transform the cape of storms into the cape of good hope.

Be encouraged. Any route to a rich life takes us through some stormy seas. If you are in the middle of a difficult time, chances are good that you're about to find a new passage to hope and freedom. If you aren't in a storm now or haven't encountered one recently, count your blessings—and then batten down the hatches, because a squall might be on its way. As we will explore in more depth throughout this book, storms are a part of life, but they don't have to cause us to abandon ship or abort the trip, even when we are forced ashore. They can be the very things that open up a new way of life to us.

We are all on different legs of the voyage. Some of us have just set out on what we feel will be the great adventure of our lives. We are full of enthusiasm and joy as we step aboard ship. Others have been on the boat for a while now, already a little tossed about by the waves, but the weather has been good and the anticipation is still high. Yet others have been severely buffeted and are not sure their craft will weather the storm. They face the very real possibility of being forced ashore. And I can imagine there are a number of brave explorers who have already rounded the cape of storms. They wondered if they would ever make it to the other side, but looking back they can see the cape of good hope shining like a jewel under sunny skies.

It was a full ten years before another Portuguese explorer, Vasco da Gama, rounded the very same cape. He went on to reach India, making him the first person to open the sea route from Europe to the East and prove that rounding the Cape of Good Hope was indeed the way to reach the riches of the East.

So we invite you, dear explorers, to sail on. Feel the sun on your back and the wind in your hair, and dare to keep going forward toward the life you long for. Or hold tightly to the mast in the middle of the tempest and know that this storm, too, shall pass, and the morning will come. Or stand on the deck and give thanks to God that you have made it safely around a cape of storms. Praise him that you are stronger now, and smile as you look to the future with irrepressible hope!

part ONE

Charting Your Course

This came... in 1714 as of direction, and also a prize
for anyone who... hundred years, calculation had made it a new prob-
accurately... for measuring longitude, but without an accurate clock it was and impossible fact 7146 pm American has
hard to a... necessary for establishing... construction and
pound prize for the discovery of longitude.

Twenty years later, a humble clock... named the

Two Fixed Points

NICOLE JOHNSON

*Because God wanted to make the unchanging nature
of his purpose very clear to the heirs of what was promised,
he confirmed it with an oath. God did this so that, by two
unchangeable things in which it is impossible for God to lie,
we who have fled to take hold of the hope offered to
us may be greatly encouraged. (Hebrews 6:17–18)*

When sailors first took to the sea, they navigated by the equator and the stars. They charted their courses by what we now understand as latitude, but they were not always accurate. They could determine with ease their positions in the north and south, but couldn't track their east and west movements. They knew they were missing information— longitude—but they had no instrument by which to measure it. This caused shipwrecks, loss of direction, and aborted voyages.

For almost two hundred years, sailors had tried to develop an accurate way of measuring longitude, but without an accurate clock it remained impossible. In 1714 Queen Anne put her hand to a parliamentary act establishing a twenty-thousand-pound prize for the discovery of longitude.

Twenty years later, a humble clockmaker changed the

world. By creating an instrument that would measure distances from east to west, he made it possible to calculate two fixed points, or two coordinates, and thus determine location anywhere in the world. Because of John Harrison, we have everything from detailed maps to Global Positioning Systems to chart our precise positions on the planet.

The writer of Hebrews gives us the same thing: two fixed points. Because God wanted to make his unchanging nature very clear to us, he gave us the latitude and longitude of the spiritual world: his character and his Word. These two fixed points never change, and therefore we can always know where he is. This gives us hope beyond measure. We can look at any circumstance and find God. He is not undeterminable in the vast sea of this world; he has given us his coordinates.

His latitude is his character. As sure as the equator circles the earth, separating north from south, God's character circles our world. His character is good, and it has never changed from the beginning of time. He called himself "I AM WHO I AM" (Exodus 3:14). Fixed and true. He will not lie; he will not go back on his Word or change his nature. He is kind, just, and loving. These aspects of his character are as precise as any degree on the equator, and we can count on them as surely as the sun comes up every morning.

But just like the piece of history mentioned above, our understanding of longitude came later. It was there all along, but it took us awhile to learn to measure it. The longitude of God is his Word. "In the beginning was the Word, and the Word was with God, and the Word was God" (John 1:1). Out of his character came his Word, his Son, who was his Promise.

He forever marked the map of our world with his Word of love. He spoke his Word into being and made provision for our sin because there would be no other way for us to know where he is. We were separated from him and we would ultimately be lost at sea without him. Christ, the Living Word of God, became our longitude.

By these two fixed points, we can always find God. On the roughest seas, in the driest seasons, in the middle of the night, or on the pier at dawn—if we look for his character and his Word, we will always find him. And interestingly enough, as we find him, we find ourselves. He gives us his coordinates so we can always find our way home.

~ *Almighty God, you made the heavens and the earth and have given us the great privilege of charting them. But thank you ever so much more for giving us the two fixed points of your character and your Word so we can always find you. When it is dark and we can't see you, remind us of where you are. When the fog rolls in and mist shrouds your face, your never-changing coordinates remind us that you are still there. Amen.*

Don't Forget the Eraser!

PATSY CLAIRMONT

~

Commit your way to the LORD. (Psalm 37:5)

Okay, so I'm a crummy course charter. Whew, I said it. I've just never been good at planning for the future— at least not without disappointment. Truthfully I find it a full-time job just trying to live in the here and now. I must say I do envy (tsk, tsk) those who have long-range goals and actually attain them. My conversations tend to be sprinkled with "I wish I would have . . ."; "If only . . ."; "Maybe next time." So if your Palm Pilot is confidently mapped out until Jesus comes, you may not want to dillydally in this devotional—which is written to give hope to flighty folks like me.

I've slowly learned along life's way to make plans in pencil and carry a fat eraser. For instance, my husband is a strong financial planner, but the fluctuating stock market a few years ago blew holes in our strategies, which reminded us that while we may make smart future decisions, life is full of twists and turns that require us to remain flexible.

Flexibility is a necessary quality of a gifted course charter. I tend to be rigid. When I was being formed in my mother's womb, I think my crankcase got wound too tight, because I get down-right cranky when my plans change. It's hard for me to adjust because I like things to work out according to my expectations. In fact, in my younger years just a minor alteration in my schedule could throw me into an emotional tailspin. Now whether that was a sign of an inflated control issue or just a clear picture of how deep my insecurity was, I'll leave up to the psychologists. How it impacted my daily existence was that I came to believe a set plan did nothing more than set me up to be disenchanted.

How does one overcome inflexibility? If we live life through enough crosswind seasons, I guarantee either we'll learn to be pliable or we'll shatter—or our rigidness will turn to bitterness. Imagine a sailboat with iron sails. Why, there would be no way to catch the winds that propel us to our destination; besides, the weight of those sails would sink our skiff.

Some years ago my hubby and I put in a bid on a tiny home. The owners accepted our offer and we were thrilled. I began making plans and mentally pictured myself in this tidy dwelling. But when we came up against a small snag with the closing, the owners used that as an excuse to jump ship. Seems a better offer had come their way. My sails hardened. We were living with my parents at the time and all of us longed for our own space. Besides, in my mind that home was my dream cottage. I fumed around for days making life unbearable for us all.

Finally, in frustration, I fell to my knees and called upon the Lord. By the time I stood up, I realized my ways are not necessarily God's ways and that his plans supercede all others, which led me to the tack of flexibility. My new, pliable sails corrected my course. That day I learned that the mainsail of flexibility is relinquishment—a lesson I've had to relearn again and again throughout my life.

Relinquishment says, above all paths, plans, and people, I

will deliberately rest in God's superintending of my life. I will chart my course to the best of my ability and watch as God fills my sails and compassionately involves himself in the direction my life ultimately takes. This assurance gives me the hope that allows me to lean in and enjoy the ride.

During our 2003 Women of Faith conference season, our gifted dramatist Nicole Johnson performed a brilliant skit about a mom who had a controlling spirit, a rebellious daughter, and a predetermined course set in place. When her plans began to unravel, the mom wrestled with God about getting into the boat of relinquishment, and even though her daughter had run away, she continued to demand to have things her way. It felt too scary for her to relax her control, lest she lose her darling daughter forever. And as often happens in life, other people don't cooperate with our charted course. After a fierce struggle with God, her daughter, and herself, the mom fell into the boat of relinquishment and eventually lifted the sail. By the close of the skit she was leaning into the wind and loving her newfound freedom in God's direction.

Whether we are talented at mapping a course or we're hesitant sailors, what will make the journey a success is our willingness to sail the course God has charted. So let's climb in the boat, grab a pencil, and—oh, yes, don't forget the eraser!

(By the way, after our house deal fell through, my husband had an unexpected job offer in another town and we moved.)

∿ Lord, teach us to chart a course and then follow your lead. May the winds of your Spirit fill our sails as we lean into you. Amen.

Birdbrain

MARILYN MEBERG

*I will lead the blind by a way they
do not know. (Isaiah 42:16 NASB)*

A few weeks ago, a couple of pigeons made their nest on a little roof over my garage door, which is not connected to the main roof. I assumed that location promised a cozy tuckaway for nest building, egg laying, and bird raising. At first I found this pigeon activity sweet. When my front door is open I hear their constant cooing as they work to perpetuate their bird breed. Now, however, they are getting on my nerves.

Here's the progression of my irritation. When I walk out my front door, I set off a flurry of protest from the pigeons, who proceed to fly wildly from their nest, missing my head by inches. Of course, I reason, they are concerned with homeland security. That's an admirable instinct. I'll respect it. So instead of going out my front door, I've made it my practice to walk to the back of my condo, go through the slider door, cross the little outdoor patio, and open the garage door, thus making my escape. I've assumed the pigeons are grateful for my display of sensitivity.

Yesterday I was sending some faxes from my little office.

The window of that office is next to the bird-dominated roof nook. I casually looked out the window just in time to see two bird eggs roll off the cement-tiled roof and splat on the walk below. I felt awful. I dashed out the front door to examine the catastrophe. There were more than two egg splats . . . there were six. Apparently the egg roll had been going on for some time. Why?

Clearly something was wrong. I pulled my ladder from the garage so I could see the nest. (The pigeons had done their wild bird-bomb when I came out the front door, so I was momentarily safe from potential attack.) I couldn't believe my eyes. No wonder the eggs kept rolling off the roof. The nest was built on a slant. I had wondered about a flat spot in that roof location and just assumed the pigeons had found one I couldn't see. I had also noticed the difficulty they always had claw-clinging to the slanted tile just before they took off to torpedo me. The slanted nest explained why the egg-laying, bird-raising routine was taking so long. They kept losing eggs. What kind of birdbrain would build a nest on a slant?

So now I've basically lost compassion for them. "If your eggs rolled off the roof once," I say, "wouldn't it occur to you there's got to be a better way? If you just took a second to peer down at the splats below, wouldn't you conclude that you might want to rethink your nest construction?" My irritation with the pigeon parents is expressed by me no longer exiting my condo through the garage. I simply adjust the straps on my helmet and march out the front door.

You may be wondering what my low-IQ pigeons have to do with charting one's course or preparing for a voyage. I realize pigeons don't have anything to do with sailing; they're probably taxing their abilities just to fly straight. But here's where I make a comparison: Any new venture, whether it's "birding" or sailing, requires sensible forethought and planning.

I read a newspaper account about two teenage boys who took their dad's sailboat out for a "quick trip" from Newport Harbor to the ocean. They figured they'd be back at the dock before Dad ever knew they had "borrowed" his boat. Once in the ocean, the quick trip was extended by a quick storm. The violent waves and fierce wind threatened to capsize the boat. Neither boy had experienced much beyond in-harbor sailing; both of them were terrified as well as unprepared. When the storm passed almost as quickly as it had come, they felt tremendous relief. Nevertheless, they'd lost sight of land and had no compass. For hours they drifted aimlessly at the whim of the wind that caught their sails. They were ultimately rescued by the Coast Guard, which their anxious father had sent out.

We would assume those two boys learned something from their dangerous and ill-prepared venture. We would assume they gained a little wisdom about sailing off into uncharted water with no prior sailing experience. But on the other hand, why would we make such an assumption? Do we not all struggle with repeating behavior we know to be unwise? Are there not many of us who mindlessly watch our eggs roll off the roof? What's the problem here?

Many of us set sail without being prepared. We lack wisdom. If we want a smooth sail, we must take the most important first step of preparedness. We need to admit we're clueless . . . and ask God for wisdom and direction for the journey.

James 1:5 says, "If you need wisdom—if you want to know what God wants you to do—ask him, and he will gladly tell you" (NLT). Now that's simple, isn't it? And as long as we're in that verse, here's a comforting line that follows the invitation to receive wisdom: "He will not resent your asking."

I suspect the implication of that line is he'd never think to call us a birdbrain.

~ *Lord Jesus, sometimes I'm clueless. May I never try to chart my own course. I need you for that. Amen.*

With All My Heart

LUCI SWINDOLL

Follow my example, as I follow the
example of Christ. (1 Corinthians 11:1)

My mother modeled hope. She trusted the Lord all day long, all the time, all my life. I don't care what the task was; she went about it with love, diligence, and ingenuity. I distinctly remember times when there wasn't quite enough food to go around . . . so she'd add grits to chili. Or she couldn't afford a suit for one of my brothers . . . so she made one. Or I didn't want to sing in the church choir because I'd rather hang out with my friends . . . so she suggested we form our own trio. (We actually wound up singing on the radio—my first job!)

Mother needed nobody to get her started on a mission; she was a one-woman army of determination. She had a calling to her family's well-being, very much like Mother Teresa, who said, "Don't wait for leaders; do it alone, person to person."

I remember a time when my father was suffering with a bout of malaria. (I didn't realize it at the time.) He missed several weeks of work, which was strange because of Daddy's extremely strong work ethic. Mother prayed for him, watched over him, cared for him, nursed him, and kept the severity of his condition to herself so as not to upset us . . . all the while settling sibling rivalries, keeping hot meals on the table, and generally giving everyone a listening ear.

The most common picture of Mother I remember is reading her Bible. She read it every day and prayed for all of us. She'd often sit in her bed and read or at the dining table where she could spread the pages open. She memorized Scripture, underlined passages, and wrote notes in the margin.

As a flippant, moody teenager, I wheeled around one day as I was going out the door to school and said something smart-alecky like, "Don't tell me you believe all that stuff in the Bible, Mother."

She raised her head, looked me square in the eye, and with the kindest, sweetest expression of assurance said, "With all my heart, honey." How was I going to give some two-bit response to *that?* So I flounced out. But in sixty-plus years I've never forgotten what Mother said or the look on her face.

There were many ways I seriously disagreed with my mother, but I could never argue with her trust or hope in the Lord. She charted the course for the whole family, and I can say without equivocation that it is she who provided the initial momentum that resulted in all three of her children winding up in Christian ministry. She demonstrated in her own life everything we needed to become strong in our faith in Christ. The Lord used Mother to guide us into the harbor of truth and to model for us how to follow him faithfully, with all our hearts.

It was one of Mother's favorite pastimes to make little books for those she loved. They were put together from fabric and scrap paper and filled with poetry, photos, and passages from the Bible. She wrote notes in them and dated each entry. She called them "Promise Books," and I can see her now taking them to church to give to various friends. In 1967 she started one for me and wrote in it almost every day until she died on February 9, 1971. I had no idea she was doing that and found it in her house after her death. It's filled with her handwriting and small paintings . . . just for me. A treasure!

One entry reads, "We can only get out of life what we see in it. It is for us to determine whether it shall be just daily drudgery or joyous service." I love that! It's so my philosophy—learned from my mother, I'm sure.

One of my favorite things about Mother was that she never stopped learning. She firmly believed that her hope in Christ was measured by how much she knew about him. If she wanted to have a meaningful life, she needed to become as intimately acquainted with God as possible.

An entry in my Promise Book on February 3, 1968, reads:

KEEP HOLDING ON TO WHAT IS RIGHT

1. Continue to keep a firm hold on my profession of faith in Christ.

2. Continue coming with courage to the throne of God to obtain mercy and spiritual strength when I need it.

3. Continue progressing toward maturity.

4. Continue filling my mind with the things above, not with things on earth.

5. Continue to find and follow God's will—what is well pleasing to Him.

6. Continue to show the same earnestness to the very end so I may enjoy my hope to the fullest.

My mother was the epitome of *continuing* on the course she set—to enjoy her hope to the fullest. What a concept!

Continue trusting God with your needs and desires. He will make a way for you to do the things you think you can't, meet the demands that seem impossible, and reap the rewards for a job well done. As Psalm 146:5 says, "Blessed is he whose help is the God of Jacob, whose hope is in the LORD his God." Much of my happiness today stems from knowing my help and my hope are in the God of Jacob—and my mother.

⌣ *Be a beacon of encouragement to me today, Lord. Show me how to continue trusting you with all my heart, and make me a blessing to those around me. Amen.*

Mission Impossible?

BARBARA JOHNSON

*He called out to them, "Friends, haven't you any
fish?" "No," they answered. He said, "Throw your
net on the right side of the boat and you will find
some." When they did, they were unable to haul the
net in because of the large number of fish. Then
the disciple whom Jesus loved said to Peter,
"It is the Lord!" (John 21:5–7)*

The little group of apostles had fished all night long
without even a nibble. Maybe it was because their
minds were someplace else, remembering the scene outside
Jerusalem when their Master had been crucified. Maybe they
were thinking of the empty tomb and then the room where
they had gathered, all the doors locked, when they suddenly
and most miraculously found Jesus, risen from the dead,
standing among them, talking to them and reassuring them—
and, most important, challenging them.

"As the Father has sent me, I am sending you," he had
said. And with that he had breathed the Holy Spirit onto
them and told them, "If you forgive anyone his sins, they are
forgiven; if you do not forgive them, they are not forgiven"
(John 20:21–23).

Can you imagine the thoughts that swirled through the disciples' heads that long, dark night as their little boat bobbed silently on the dark waves of the Sea of Galilee? No wonder they hadn't caught any fish! They probably hadn't even planned to catch any. Instead, the former fishermen may have returned to the water, their home away from home, slipping back into the old, familiar routine simply so they could think. Maybe as the long hours dragged on they recounted what they had witnessed. Twice since his crucifixion Jesus had come to them, suddenly appearing in their midst when all the doors were locked. Maybe they talked about what they would do next.

"I am sending *you*," he had told them.

The mission Jesus had given them seemed impossible. But then, he had obviously done the impossible himself, and he had empowered them with the Holy Spirit. So it must have seemed possible that now *they* could do the impossible too. Surely they felt a lot of excitement as they thought about these things. In all probability their excitement was mixed with a healthy portion of fear. But there must have been something else. Remembering what they had seen, they also had to be full of hope.

Maybe that's why they heeded the man calling to them from the shore. How silly, how illogical it would have seemed just a few days earlier to have thought that simply moving their nets to the other side of the boat would make a difference. Surely, under normal circumstances, they would have scoffed at the man and ignored his advice. But not now. Now they were becoming attuned to illogical ideas becoming reality. So they moved their nets to the other side of the boat, and within moments the nets were so full of fish they couldn't lift them. The apostle John didn't have to squint toward the man on shore any longer to know who he was. He looked at all those flipping, flapping, shimmering fish and immediately knew without a doubt what had happened. He shouted to Peter, "It is the Lord!"

Anyone but Peter might have hung back. After all, when the pressure had mounted on Jesus, Peter had denied even knowing him. So you might think he would be embarrassed, humiliated, afraid. Instead Peter impulsively dived overboard, in too much of a hurry to be with Jesus to wait for the boat to bring him to shore.

Jesus cooked breakfast for the apostles over a fire he had built beside the water. As he fed them, he told them again what he wanted them to do: "Feed my lambs. . . . Take care of my sheep." He wasn't really talking about livestock, of course. He was talking about people. About you and me. And what he fed the apostles that morning wasn't just bread and fish; he was serving up a big helping of hope.

There was work to be done, and he was sending them out to do it, empowering them with the force that would change the world.

The Gospel of John ends with that story of Jesus giving the disciples their assignment. But as Eugene Petersen wrote in *The Message* as he introduced Acts, the New Testament book that follows the Gospel of John, "The story of Jesus doesn't end with Jesus. It continues in the lives of those who believe in him. . . . Which also means, of course, in *us.*"

Do you sense that God wants to send you out on a divine mission? Do you feel Jesus urging you to feed his lambs, to take care of his sheep? Maybe the challenge seems too big, too scary, too illogical. If so, perhaps you should follow the disciples' lead. Get away for a while to a place where you can think and consider the steps you might take. And be alert to the voice calling from the shoreline of your mind, urging you to try something new, something different. Then take a big breath, draw in the gift of the Holy Spirit that has been given to you, and dive into the task with hope.

~ *Dear Jesus, you feed me with your love, change me with your fire, and fill me with your empowering hope. Send me out, Lord, to do your will. I am ready. Amen.*

God Knows

THELMA WELLS

You say, "I choose the appointed time; it is I who judge uprightly." (Psalm 75:2)

One day I was sitting at my computer perusing my e-mail when a whale of an idea came dashing onto my screen. From the big blue background leaped smartly designed copy: MASTER'S DIVINITY SCHOOL AND GRADUATE SCHOOL OF DIVINITY. I stopped and stared at it for a few minutes while something within said, "Apply. Get your master's."

Apply? Get your master's? That means work! That means study and sacrifice and reading and writing and all that stuff I don't like to do. I never intended to study in a school situation again. It was over, I thought. But I kept hearing, "Apply. Get your master's."

So I applied. The disclaimer declared that it would be several days before I would get a response to my request. But within the hour I had a reply: "Congratulations! You have been accepted into the graduate school at Master's Divinity School and Graduate School of Divinity." What was I to do now?!

My heart was shuddering like the motor of a boat suddenly thrown into full throttle. I was frightened! When I called my children and told my husband, they were all happy for me. I, on the other hand, was wondering what in the world I had done to myself. Studying, reading, writing . . . oh my goodness!

I got busy putting all my books, articles, and other projects together to send to the school to see if I could get credits added to my degree plan. I was more than a little disappointed when I learned that graduate school does not give credits. I would actually have to take—and pass—all the courses if I planned to graduate! Little did I know that God was sending me on a great voyage. When I set sail with my application, he was already calling, "Bon voyage!"

After receiving several calls from school officials asking if I would consider writing curriculum for the school, I knew something was brewing. The most startling call was from the president, Dr. Dennis Frey, who said he had been praying about starting a Women's Issues division and wanted to announce to me that this division was a new reality that very day. He continued, "Congratulations, Sister Wells! You have just become a full professor at Master's Divinity School and Graduate School of Divinity. We're using your book and Bible study video, *Girl, Have I Got Good News for You!* The course title is Biblical Template for Counseling Hurting Women."

My mouth flew open wide enough for a seagull to fly in. "Dr. Frey," I protested, "I don't deserve this. I don't have a master's or any other postgraduate degree." The compassionate educator said, "We are looking for people like you who love the Lord and have the ability to communicate." In other words, he was saying that I don't have a master's, but I have the Master, who qualified me by his anointing. I was in the Dallas airport when I got the call, so I couldn't scream and dance like I wanted to.

The next mouth-wide-open, seagull moment came when I got another call from Dr. Frey asking me if I planned to graduate in 2003, and if so, would I be the commencement speaker? *I don't have time for this,* I reasoned. *Why can't I have two years to graduate like the rest of the world?* But again I heard the inner prompting: "Just do it." I agreed to graduate and speak. Perhaps I enjoy trying to paddle out of torrents.

In my heart I had hoped to get a higher degree than a bachelor's someday; I just had not told anyone. God knew! In my heart I love learning the Bible. God knew that too! In my heart I have always enjoyed sharing my knowledge with people who wanted to learn. God knew. At the appointed time, God pulled me on board and gunned the engines for this academic voyage.

It's amazing to me how God knows our every desire, even unexpressed or unconscious. He longs to give us our most secret desires. I stand amazed at a God who gives us time, energy, space, enthusiasm, tenacity, health, strength, and hope and then works things out for us in such unorthodox ways. He does it because *God knows.*

You may have a secret desire in your heart that you haven't shared with anyone. Maybe it's still a secret from yourself! Well, don't be surprised when the Lord of the voyage sets you in the ship *Much Desire* and lands you on the Coast of Hope Realized.

~ *Captain of the voyage, you know everything. It should never surprise us when you do the things you do, but it does. Praise you that even the minutest thought that flickers in our mind catches your loving attention. All our hopes are marked on your map for our lives, and in your perfect wisdom you appoint the time for every move forward. Thanks, God. I'm glad you know. Amen.*

Just Do It

NICOLE JOHNSON

For everything that was written in the past was written to teach us, so that through endurance and the encouragement of the Scriptures we might have hope. (Romans 15:4)

It's been a long time since I've ridden my bike, but I don't think it would take me long at all to remember how. In fact, just throwing my leg over to the other side, sitting down on the seat, and putting my hands on the handlebars would probably do it. It would all come back to me.

Physiologists tell us this is muscle memory. Your muscles learn just like your mind does. You don't forget how to ride a bike physically, because your muscles remember. You train your body and it holds that training, just like when you study for a test and your mind remembers the information. Or used to, before aspartame.

Interestingly, there is such a thing as emotional memory as well. Things that have happened in the past, good and bad, remain in our emotional memory. And we have the unique ability to train our emotional memory to keep hoping, so that, just like riding a bike, we never forget how.

When we're starting out on a new venture, it's normal to

feel both excitement and anxiety. We try to look forward and figure out how things can work out well, but we can't see ahead, so we get scared. We sit on the dock, worrying that when the time comes to hoist the sail we'll forget how . . . and we'll be lost at sea with no rescue in sight.

Perhaps the best way to handle prevoyage jitters is not to try to see the future, but to look to the past. To remember all that has gone before and all the times God has filled our sails and brought us safely back to harbor.

In the Old Testament God was constantly calling his people to remember. He would say, "Look back at the past. When you were staring at a wall of water in front of you and an army coming up behind you, do you remember what happened? When you were in the wilderness with nothing to eat, do you remember who fed you? Build up your muscle memory of hope by looking back at the way I have always provided for you."

Where has God met you before when you thought you were alone? How has he shown himself faithful to you when you were lost? How many times did the money come or the help arrive or the comfort appear when you needed it the most? Stop trying to muster up hope for what's ahead, when you can look back and be reassured. You won't fear the future as much when you recognize and acknowledge his faithfulness in the past.

When it comes to trusting God, or putting our hope in him, the Nike ad wins the day: "Just do it." We learn more about trust only by trusting. We grow in our hope only by hoping. None of these jewels comes to us by simply reading or thinking about it. We have to get on board and sail out to find the treasure.

If God has come through for you in the past, and it's pretty safe to say he has, then the memory will still be there. Let it fuel your hope. Let it whisper in your ear that this time is just like the last time when God came through, and you can trust him. Let him remind you that he will be faithful once again, because he is God. Trust, trust, and, yes—trust.

Just because you haven't hoped in a while or trusted recently doesn't mean you don't know how. You just have to take your hope out of yourself and put it back in God. Just like you have done many times before. You don't forget how. Just throw your leg over to the other side of the bike, sit down on the seat of remembering, put your hands on the handlebars of hope, and it will all come back to you.

~ *Father, when we're afraid, give us the wisdom to look back instead of around or ahead. Help us to see your faithful hand so clearly in the past that we have confidence in your presence through whatever lies ahead. Amen.*

Packing with Care

SHEILA WALSH

❧

We have not stopped praying for you and asking
God to fill you with the knowledge of his will through
all spiritual wisdom and understanding. And we pray
this in order that you may live a life worthy of the Lord and
may please him in every way: bearing fruit in every good work,
growing in the knowledge of God. (Colossians 1:9–10)

When I was fourteen years old, I set off on a weekend adventure with two of my friends from school. We were working toward an annual award that is given out by Prince Phillip, Queen Elizabeth's husband, to students who have accomplished four years of community service and survival challenges. Our quest was to survive for three days in the beautiful, if freezing, terrain of the west coast of Scotland. We would stay in youth hostels at night, but we had to carry food with us to prepare for ourselves outdoors—no trips to McDonald's!

We discussed what each of us would bring. Moira said that she would bring food for breakfast, Linda said she would do lunch, and I volunteered for dinner. We set off early in the morning with our backpacks full of what we would need until we returned home safely to our families. Our teacher drove us out into the countryside and dropped us off with a map. He showed us where he would pick us up in three days. We were so excited!

After we had walked for at least a mile, we decided we were hungry. (Scottish girls are always hungry!) As Moira hunted in her sack for what would be our breakfast, Linda and I lit a fire. She tried to get it started by rubbing wood together until I dug in my pocket and produced matches. Moira got out a little fry pan and some sausages. The smell of cooking meat crackling in the open air was glorious. After a good breakfast we set off again. It was an unusually mild day and we made good headway before we stopped for lunch. Then we cleaned our plates again and trotted off. We knew we had to get to the youth hostel before six in the evening.

About three in the afternoon it started to rain. Scottish rain is very wet. It's wetter than American rain. By the time we got to our destination, we were soaked through.

"I hope you planned for a big dinner," Linda said.

"Absolutely!" I replied. "We have ham and beans and then whipped caramel custard."

They went off to book beds for the night as I headed to a table outside to prepare my gastronomic feast. But there was a snag. I hadn't brought a can opener, and my ham and my beans were in cans. I tried everything. I tried banging them on a rock hoping one would split open, to no avail. When the girls reappeared I relayed the sad news.

"Well, I hope you have a lot of caramel custard," Moira said.

"I do! I do!" I assured her.

"How are you going to mix it?" Linda asked.

"Aha! I will put the powder and the milk in this plastic sack and shake it till it's blended," I announced with a triumphant tone.

"And how long does it take to set?" Moira inquired.

It was then that I realized I had no bowl, so I had to stand holding the plastic sack for forty-five minutes until the custard set. I was not prepared!

Charting our course spiritually requires preparation and wisdom. It is one thing to find yourself in a field with a can of beans and no opener; it's quite another to find yourself stranded on your journey with no spiritual resources. We know that our final destination is our eternal home with God our Father, but he has provided supplies for us to take with us through this earthly part of our journey.

I have begun the practice of committing God's Word to heart again. I have made worship a part of my daily life as opposed to a service reserved for Sunday or Wednesday night. We are called to live a life worthy of the Lord, bearing fruit in every good work and growing in the knowledge of God. As we prepare for our voyage, let's carefully check our packs and make sure that the resources we need are tucked in there, for we don't know what the terrain or the weather might be like.

⌒ *Father, thank you for your companionship and your provision on this journey. Grant me wisdom to be prepared and to chart my course with care. Amen.*

Hope and Humor

MARILYN MEBERG

~

*So I pray that God, who gives you hope, will keep you
happy and full of peace. (Romans 15:13 NLT)*

I cannot imagine setting out on life's seas without my
humor survival kit. Without it the voyage would be
deadly dull as well as without hope. I find it interesting that
Romans 15:13 combines the words *hope, happy,* and *peace*—
all in one thought clump. I interpret that to mean that without hope you can forget being happy and you might as well
drop the idea of peace. The presence of hope opens the portals
to happiness and peace.

Hope is defined as a confident expectation. That means I
haven't got what I'm hoping to get yet, but I'm expecting to get it
any day now. When I live in expectation (hope), I'm not limited
to my present circumstances. I'm expecting these circumstances
to change or become more manageable—or I'm confident I'll be
enabled to see them in a more positive light. It is possible to
change the lens through which I view my circumstances.

My favorite lens is humor. I want to see the funny side of
life in spite of the circumstances. That doesn't mean I deny the
seriousness of what's going on; I simply add a humorous

dimension to it. Doing so brings me a measure of happiness, and that produces peace.

One of those little, not-so-serious lens changes occurred last Monday. I had been mildly obsessing about how to get ten decorator pillows and two queen pillows and shams to the post office for mailing to Frisco, Texas. If I put them all in a box, I wouldn't be able to fit the box into my too-small, impractical car. If I tried corralling them in my arms to get from my car to the post office, I was sure to leave a trail of uncooperative pillows in the parking lot. The challenge of getting the pillow community to the post office counter for mailing seemed a daunting task.

As I noodled this I was struck with an unexpected flash of brilliance. I would put the shams and queen pillows into my garment bag, stuff the other pillows into my black roller suitcase, drive to the post office, and effortlessly glide up to the counter without losing any pillows. Then I'd simply "unpack" the pillows for the post people to box and mail. Yes!

As I entered the post office with my garment bag slung over my shoulder and my suitcase in tow, it occurred to me that I presented a peculiar image. Taking in the quizzical stares cast in my direction, I cheerfully asked, "Is this the Palm Springs airport?"

No one laughed or even smiled. The postal clerk at the end of the counter said in a testy monotone, "No, ma'am, you're in the United States Post Office."

"That'll work," I said, adjusting my garment bag and getting in line. Everyone carefully avoided looking at me from that moment on.

I found the whole experience incredibly amusing and giggled all the way home. When I told Luci about everyone's mirthless response, she reminded me that we live in a retirement community where it is all too probable some of our members may not know the difference between the airport and the post office.

The ability to adjust our lens and see our experiences as carrying potential for occasional hope-radiating laughs is easier for most of us when we are not hurting deeply. When loss seems imminent and our security is threatened, many of us lose the inclination to laugh. And when we lose the inclination to laugh, we have probably lost hope. When we lose hope, we lose happiness and peace.

I well remember the sense of bleak hopelessness I felt one afternoon as I slowly circled the parking lot at Hogue Hospital in an effort to find a parking space. I had let my husband, Ken, out at the entrance for another chemo treatment. From my perspective, there wasn't a whit of good in those treatments; they only made him nauseous and weak. I hated it for him.

Finally, a frail little man pulled out of his parking space and inched away. I slid into his spot feeling no hope, no happiness, and no peace. If anyone had dared to smile at me, I'd probably have snarled and hissed.

That evening as Ken and I were reading the paper, he looked over at me and said, "You know, babe, if no one ever died, it would become increasingly difficult to find a parking space." It took me a minute, but that off-the-wall, absurd humor I so loved in Ken settled into my interior being until it touched the spot where hope lay limp and obscure on the floor of my soul. I began to smile. Ken winked at me and went back to reading the paper. Hope slowly surfaced. Humor nudged it into motion.

Psalm 31:24 consoles us, "Be strong and take courage, all you who put your hope in the LORD!" (NLT). Our hope is authored and anchored in God. God has created within all of us a capacity for humor. We may not create it, but we can appreciate it. Humor restores our balance, relieves some dread, and lightens our load.

I'm convinced that when we are hope-anchored in God and live with the good medicine the humor lens provides, our sail through life will be less stormy.

～ *Thank you, Jesus, that our anchor holds. Amen.*

Queen of Charts

PATSY CLAIRMONT

*See, I am sending an angel ahead of you to guard
you along the way and to bring you to the place
I have prepared. (Exodus 23:20)*

Luci Swindoll has to be the queen of charting a course. She has a way of making the preparation for a trip seem every bit as exciting and inviting as the journey itself. Luci's friends have the joy of watching her chart her trip for months prior to her leaving for the four corners of the world. Peeking in on Luci's strategy would be like trailing Julia Child through the grocery store as she selects the finest produce for a luscious meal she's about to create, or observing Thomas Kinkade choose a palette for his next canvas of lights, or sitting in on a practice session of the Brooklyn Tabernacle Choir. When it comes to Luci's preparedness, she's a piece of work.

I, on the other hand, tend to be piecemeal in my approach to upcoming events. I'm not sure what it is about me, but I don't truly focus in on my needs for a journey until I pack. And I don't pack until the night before the morning I leave. It's then I realize I'm out of toothpaste, I'm down to my last pair of pantyhose (and they have a run the length of the

Mississippi River), I'm missing a button off my jacket, and I don't have enough meds to last through my journey. Then the panic begins as I rush east and my dear hubby runs west in our attempts to restock my suitcase.

Then there's my purse. When I check to make sure I have my photo ID, I realize I still have my last airline ticket, room keys, receipts, gum wrappers, and loose peppermint candies stuffed willy-nilly in my bag. And speaking of tickets, I'm never quite sure where I've tucked the current ones, which means a mad scramble will ensue as we dismantle the house in search of my latest designated "safe place." (Can you imagine how relieved my husband is to get me out the door?)

Luci not only has everything she requires way ahead of time, but she often takes doubles in case her friends need some. She actually makes up an inventory list of her suitcase contents, while I can't remember where I put my suitcase after the last trip I took. I've always thought "trip" defines my attempts to prepare, because I sure do a lot of tripping about as I try to head out of my house into an unsuspecting world.

Here's what's funny: My mom was just like Luci. Mom had charting a course down to a science. Whether it was a picnic at the park or a trip to Mamaw's house, Mom spent days and sometimes weeks in preparation. And I don't remember ever having needed something that Mom didn't have at her fingertips. Speaking of fingertips, for the life of me I can't remember to make a nail appointment in advance, which often leaves me filing madly in the car on the way to the airport with a broken emery board that I found floating around in the recesses of my purse.

So would you hire me to equip your ship? Hardly, although I believe I'm improving, because last week I made it all the way to my hotel before I missed anything. It was my pants. Gratefully I was wearing a pair that would fill in for the ones stranded in my closet at home.

I really do understand the importance of a well-established plan, a defined course, and a stocked galley. Those who are masters of all of the above have blessed me with their thoughtful preparations, and I've been taking notes. But where, oh where, did I put them?

〜 *Lord, a number of us folks fall short of a full galley. We know you are the ultimate supplier, but we are also aware that we have a responsibility to you, others, and ourselves. Would you teach us what it is we need to pre-think and prepare so that we're ready for the challenges on life's high seas? And thank you that when we forget something vital to our journey, you are merciful and provisional. Amen.*

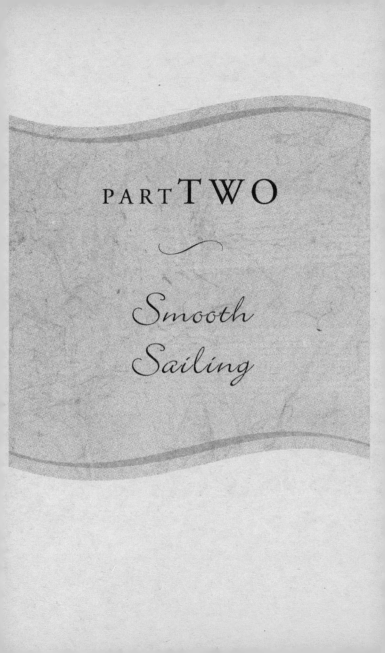

PART TWO

Smooth Sailing

All Knotted Up

NICOLE JOHNSON

We have this hope as an anchor for the soul,
firm and secure. (Hebrews 6:19)

I've always thought knots were nuisances. It was hard for me to see a knot as a positive thing. Before a big test in school, I would get a knot in my stomach. If I wasn't careful with a delicate necklace, the chain would get a knot in it, and that was a disaster. Even early on, while learning to tie my shoes, sometimes the careful bow I was trying to tie would end up in a knot that I couldn't get undone, and I would have to ask for help.

I once read about the challenge of a knot devised by a king named Gordius that was cut by Alexander the Great. And to this day when we encounter a problem that it seems impossible to find a solution for, we call it a Gordian knot. Naturally I came to the conclusion that knots were not so swift.

Then I went sailing.

That's when I discovered what the Boy Scouts have known all along: Knots are important. They aren't just what happens when something goes wrong. They aren't just the result of an unfortunate accident with a piece of string. When used with knowledge and skill, knots are one of the keys to smooth sailing because they provide security. This is the job of a good knot.

On a boat there are lots of ropes—but these ropes are called lines. Many lines have one function and purpose: to be tied to something secure. In order to be secure, each line must be tied to something fixed on the other end by a very strong knot. While bows are pretty, they are not strong enough for our deepest connections. Sailors would never use bows, as they come untied too easily. They are a great way to make something cute, but not such a good way to make it secure.

Before you tie a knot, you need to make sure that what you're tying it to is strong enough to hold it secure. The strength of a good knot comes from the thing to which it is tied. You can tie the best knot in the world on the end of the mainsail line, but if it's tied to a life jacket, it will not give you much hope. The life jacket is a good thing, but it is not strong enough to support the mainsail, and therefore the strong knot is rendered useless or seen as silly or a pain in the neck to try to untie.

Our lives have a lot of lines as well. It is easy for those lines to get knotted up about all sorts of things, with bad knots in the middle that keep us from sailing with ease. These obstacles come from tying ourselves to things to which we should not be tied: false obligations, guilt feelings, or our own fears. We can learn to untie those knots and retie them to the right things—the things that make us secure and set us free at the same time.

Hope runs along lines that are tied with strong knots to the right things: to an anchor or to the dock or to a cleat. These things bring hope because they are secure. We don't have to worry; we can trust. But this means that the lines cannot be tied to another person. They cannot be tied to any of our possessions. They cannot be tied to our performance. No, when we try to tie the lines of our lives to those things, we end up in knots, feeling insecure. And the whole idea is to be sailing.

So the best knot we can tie is to Christ. That is the line that makes us secure and sets us free at the same time. He is the anchor and the cleat for the lines of our lives. This is the reason the Bible calls hope our spiritual lifeline. Because when the line of our lives is tied to something strong enough to support us, we have great hope. When we tie the mainsail of our lives to Christ, the line is made secure by the strong knot of his love, and it will not pull loose. He is holding it tight on the other end, and that gives us security. He directs our lives with the wind of his great love, and we get glorious hope freely and generously from him.

⌣ *Oh, Captain, our Captain, show us how to tie the right knots. Show us how to untangle the mess we've made in the lines of our lives. Give us wisdom before we tie any knots, lest they be tied to things that will not hold. Make us secure and set us free by the strong knot of your love tied to the anchor of hope. Amen.*

The Optimism Equation

MARILYN MEBERG

It was by faith that Noah built an ark to save his family from the flood. (Hebrews 11:7 NLT)

I love cows. There is something peacefully optimistic about cows. They have well-ordered lives with a seemingly clear sense of what the next step is to be in their daily routine. When they finish eating they don't fret about what to do with themselves when the food is consumed. They immediately settle into the purposeful activity of chewing their cud. Later they give milk for the nutritional perpetuation of life, whether for a kitten or my grandson. They don't worry about whether their milk is well received or if the latest "Got Milk?" campaign furthers consumption. The cows simply do what cows do: eat, chew their food, and give milk. Looks like smooth sailing to me.

In spite of the sense of peace cows pass on to me, I've never quite gotten past my distaste for the cud-chewing part of their routine. The cud is food regurgitated from the stomach for the purpose of a "re-chew." That re-chew goes on for hours. I've never noticed a grimace of displeasure registered on the faces of the cows I've studied, but it does seem admirable that they press on in spite of the continual regurgitation they deal with each day. Quite frankly, I'm impressed by their optimistic attitudes.

There is something universally appealing about an optimistic attitude. That appeal goes beyond the optimism of a man who gets married at ninety-three and buys a house near a school. At a deep level we are comforted and encouraged by optimistic people because optimism implies we have control over our circumstances. We would like to believe circumstances will fall into line based on the power of our positive thinking.

There is, however, a subtle problem with that brand of optimism. It may be nothing more than the creation of our own reality as we wish it to be. Faith as the Bible explains it emphasizes what God does, not what I wish for, however purely or fervently. Faith is the confident belief in the person of God and his sovereign plan for my life, and that his ways are not my ways. There may be nothing wrong with "my way," but it may not be "his way." Therefore, whatever I hope for or believe I can achieve needs to be given over to him to do as he wills. That's an optimistic truth because the burden is off me and my limited human thinking.

Like faith, hope is also part of the optimism equation. Hope is the expectation of fulfillment that is anchored in God's promise to meet my need. Hope is not based on my emotional or mental determination. It is rooted in God. Quite simply, we are optimistic because we have faith in whom we have placed our hope.

Let's go back a few centuries and look at Noah's dad, Lamech, as an example of one who knew how the faith-hope-optimism principle works. Genesis 5:28 says, "When Lamech was 182 years old, his son Noah was born" (NLT). With Noah's birth Lamech said, "He will bring us relief from the painful labor of farming this ground that the LORD has cursed" (v. 29 NLT). What was Lamech talking about? Was he too old to know? He lived another 595 years, had a bunch more kids, and died at the age of 777. When Noah was born, Lamech was still a youngster. If his prophecy didn't come from senility, then what was its source? Its source was God.

Lamech had faith in all he knew and had experienced with Jehovah God. Therefore, when God gave Noah the seemingly absurd orders to build a boat in the middle of the desert in preparation for the Flood, Lamech became an optimistic cheerleader to his son. You can imagine the public ridicule the boat project inspired. Noah needed his dad's faith-filled enthusiasm. It wasn't coming from anyone else.

There have been many times when I've benefited from Luci Swindoll's optimistic cheerleading. A number of years ago we were speaking together at a conference on Mackinac Island. This charming island has no means of entrance or exit except by boat or plane. The morning we were to leave, the island was fogged in. The pilot scheduled to fly us to our connection in Detroit said sleepily at 5 A.M., "Can't fly in this weather." I looked at Luci and said, "Well, baby, give up going home . . . we can't get off the island and our flight to Palm Springs will leave without us."

"Nonsense," Luci replied cheerfully. "I'll bet you breakfast we get off the island, make all our connections, and get home on schedule."

"Throw in lunch, Pollyanna! We ain't goin' nowhere—and if we do I'll pay for every meal today."

I should have known better. Luci swung into action. Within minutes we were making our laborious way to a boat dock by means of a horse-drawn carriage. (It was either too early for the horse or he'd had pizza the night before; I had to breathe through a "customer blanket" to survive his rear-end pollution.) We then leaped from the carriage to the bobbing taxi boat, whose job it was to get us to shore for our commuter bus to the airport.

"You're amazing, Luci," I said as I paid for her breakfast at the airport. "There's no way in the world I thought we'd get here on time."

"I know, Marilyn," Luci chuckled. "Your problem is you need to become a Christian so you'd have a little hope for life's challenges."

I would have flung a biscuit at her, but I'd recovered from the horse pollution and was hungry. Besides, I greatly appreciated her cheerleading optimism when mine disappeared.

Sometimes I think I'd benefit from going out in a field somewhere and chewing my cud. I hate the idea, but there are times I need to do a "re-chew" on the attitudes I swallow.

~ *Thank you, Jesus, for helping me re-chew my attitudes. Sailing is smoother when I invite your help. Amen.*

Spare Parts and Big Feet

BARBARA JOHNSON

~

I wait for the LORD, my soul waits, and in
his word I put my hope. (Psalm 130:5)

ecause of my battle with cancer, it's been a while since
I've appeared onstage at a Women of Faith conference.
If you've attended one in years gone by, however, I hope you
remember me as presenting at least a marginally put-together
appearance when I was a regular part of the speaker team: my
hair combed, makeup camouflaging my wrinkles, and a colorful outfit helping me hide a few extra pounds under the spot-
lights. (Okay, so the buttons were probably held on with safety
pins, and my usual "bracelet" was a bunch of rubber bands I'd
picked up somewhere, but I always tried to look good—at
least from a distance.)

If that's the image of me you remember, then you would
have been shocked to have seen me during my first two
years of recovery. Most of my hair was shaved off in the very
first week of my cancer ordeal because I had to undergo
brain surgery. And the hair that escaped the surgical scalp-
ing soon fell out due to the chemo. Other medication
caused some swelling and weight gain, but I have to admit

there was a pleasant sub-side effect to *that* side effect: My face rounded out into a nice, smooth ball that took out all my wrinkles!

I was managing to keep a pretty good attitude about the whole experience until, after the first round of chemo, I fell down and knocked out my front tooth!

Lord, I fumed at the Great Physician as I scowled into the mirror, *it's not enough that I'm bald and bloated, but I had to knock my tooth out too?!*

My dentist made me a temporary bridge, but he couldn't do a permanent repair until another health problem was resolved. So for more than a year I had to make sure all my spare parts were in place whenever I ventured outside my home. I had to check that both my wig and my fake tooth were on straight before I dared go out in public. I was afraid I'd see someone who'd known me in my former life and scare her into convulsions!

To make matters worse, my feet were chronically swollen. I complained to my doctor that all my shoes were too tight, hoping he might adjust my medication, but instead he told me, "Just buy bigger shoes!"

My pal Lynda heard about that directive and, always eager to help, showed up at my door bearing a little gift for me. Actually I should say she brought a *big* gift: her husband's size-thirteen house shoes! As if the slippers' size alone didn't make them large enough to fill my entire living room, they were shaped like moose heads—with antlers extending out to either side.

I wouldn't even think of wearing them—until Lynda insisted that I slip them on. I could have fit both feet *and* my arms up to my elbows inside them, so there was no question that they had plenty of capacity, no matter how big my feet planned to swell. It was impossible to walk in them; I could only shuffle. But for some strange reason, in the evenings when Bill and I were finished with the day's office work and doctor appointments, I would find myself settling back in my easy chair—my hair off and my tooth out—*wanting* to slip my feet into those ridiculous moose heads. They *were* warm and cozy, and there was another benefit: Just looking at them propped up on the footrest made me giggle.

It was in those private moments that the most unexpected sense of peace would sweep over me. I'd sit there thinking, *Here I am, still battling cancer, still sporting a hairstyle more appropriate for a marine than a grandmother, my front tooth out and my wig two rooms away—and yet I have an overwhelming feeling that all is well. As ridiculous as it might be to someone else, I feel like I'm in heaven on earth.*

The first time the attitude came over me, it was so surprising and so strong that I had to pause a moment to think about it, remembering Oscar Wilde's remark: "We are all in the gutter, but some of us are looking at the stars." That's exactly where I found myself. Looking out from a life that had been brutally kicked off course, I was still able to see God's gleaming promises of heavenly hope twinkling in the distance. And in those moments, I didn't worry about the medical procedures I faced or the gap in my smile or the beams of light bouncing off my bald head.

The tiniest pinprick of hope twinkling in our lives can restore us and empower us. As some wise person once said, human beings can live about forty days without food, about three days without water, about eight minutes without air . . . but only one second without hope. And that one little second of hope can work wonders.

Of course, the *next* second may bring some new adventure entirely. One evening last December, Bill and I had settled in for a quiet night of relaxing. We turned off the porch light, let the answering machine handle the phone calls, and planned to watch a movie and go to bed early. I'd pulled on my favorite well-worn robe, taken out my tooth, slipped off my wig, stuck my feet into the moose heads, and curled up in my easy chair when we heard a sudden commotion in the front yard.

Bill peeked through the blinds. I saw him draw in a breath, but before he could speak a voice rang out: "Hi, Bill!"

He'd been spotted. Then the singing started.

"Happy birthday to you . . . Happy birthday, dear Barbara . . ."

Some of my friends, bearing a cake and gifts, had come for an impromptu birthday party!

~ *Oh, Jesus, thank you for the abiding peace that comes as a side effect of our hope in you. And thank you for friends who don't care if my smile is potholed, my head is bald, and my feet are big. Amen.*

Live the Life Out of It!

LUCI SWINDOLL

~

This is the day the LORD has made; let us rejoice
and be glad in it. (Psalm 118:24)

My wonderful brother Orville and I were talking a few days ago. He's seventy-one (thirteen months older than I) and still traveling all over the world, writing books, speaking, and preaching like there's no tomorrow. We were comparing notes about growing older as siblings, and I asked him how he was feeling these days with so many duties and obligations staring him in the face.

"Well," he said, "I walk, eat right, take naps, and I have to say, I feel great. I still do everything I want . . . but a bit slower." I could identify with that. Then he said something that sunk right into my heart and planted itself there. I keep thinking about it. "Sis, I plan to enjoy every day God gives me and *live the life out of it*. As long as I'm alive, there's hope in the Lord and every single day is a gift."

Preach on, Bubba! During the best or the worst of times, Orville lives this way and always has. He doesn't spend time accumulating regrets about what he might have done or fear over what could happen. He doesn't miss the joy God gives him moment by moment. I can hardly think of him without envisioning his head thrown back, laughing uproariously about nothing. He loves life like few people I've ever known.

Orville truly lives as if this *is* the day the Lord has made. He rejoices and is glad in it. He inspires me. Notice in Psalm 118 that the rejoicing comes *before* the gladness. The rejoicing is in God making the day, not in our finding something to be glad about. That might seem insignificant, but it says everything. Sometimes we think we can't be happy (or "glad," in this case) until something happens that evokes that feeling. But the gift of the day itself is enough to make us happy. The trick is seeing it. And the ability to see it lies in hope. Our hope in the Lord helps us recognize that there is gladness tucked into the nooks and crannies of every twenty-four-hour period if we pay attention.

When hope is threaded throughout our days, every moment has its own life, its own possibility for joy, happiness, and love. Just ask someone who's dying—every day of life takes on new meaning. Talk to someone who's lost a loved one. They would give anything to have had a few more minutes with the one now gone. Living the life out of a day means entering fully into whatever comes along the way, big or little, significant or trivial.

At times, especially when our expectations are not met, we miss so much of life's reward and blessing. We have some notion of what will make us truly happy and we stubbornly hang on to that. Meanwhile, we waste our lives longing for something that doesn't exist . . . and never will.

In December of 2002 I took a fantastic voyage to Antarctica. The trip was full of surprises and was beyond my expectations at every turn. I was out on deck one evening standing apart from all my other shipmates, talking to the Lord. With my camera strapped around my neck and wearing my red parka, skullcap, and gloves, I could feel the cold air on my face and was happy as a clam. At that moment, I thought, *I hope I see a whale.* With that as a springboard, I asked the Lord to please surface one right in front of me. And why not? I knew it wasn't too much to ask, because he can do anything. He's in charge of the fish of the sea, and nothing's impossible for him.

I poised my camera and waited for a whale to pop up. Time passed. And passed. And passed. No whale in sight. As I was about ready to lower my camera in disappointment, we approached an enormous iceberg the size of Manhattan. On it was a darling little penguin, looking straight at me. It was as if that penguin said, "What about me? I'm dressed in a tuxedo and ready for my picture to be taken. I know I'm not a whale, but don't you think I'm cute? Take me."

He was posing. So I focused my camera on the penguin. As a larger part of the iceberg came into view, I realized there was a whole rookery of penguins just waiting to be photographed. Think of what I would have missed had I held out for the whale!

Sometimes, the focus of our hope is on something so preconceived or well defined that we miss the pleasures *God* has in store for us—things that will cause us to be glad and experience unexpected happiness. How much wiser we are when we live the life out of every day, recognizing all God gives us in the moment. We risk missing some of his greatest gifts simply by looking past them while waiting for something bigger or more dramatic or more exciting to show up.

Someday we'll be on that "other" shore, and today will be gone. Until then, take my advice: Don't wait for the whales. Take the penguins.

~ *Open my eyes to my surroundings, Lord. Give me the ability to see with my soul so that I don't miss anything you have for me. I want to be totally aware, awake, and hopeful on my voyage through this life. Amen.*

The Language of Hope

BARBARA JOHNSON

~

A cheerful heart is good medicine. (Proverbs 17:22)

It wasn't the brightest thing to do, I know. But when you're cooped up in the house day after day recovering from cancer, you sometimes have to find new ways to entertain yourself.

Bill had bought himself a pair of white tennis shoes, and after a few days I noticed that the shoelaces were looking a little grubby. Not having anything else to do (like I said, I was desperate for some sort of entertainment), I decided I would surprise him by giving his shoelaces a bath. So that night after he'd changed into his pajamas and house slippers, I sneaked the shoes into the laundry room, slipped out the laces, and put them in a pan of bleach to soak overnight.

The next morning, the shoelaces had turned to cream of wheat. There was nothing left in the pan that had any shape at all. It was just a bowl full of goo. (Moral of the story: Never soak *anything* in straight bleach.) I stood there looking at the shoelace slurry, and a dozen scenarios ran through my mind about how I would tell Bill what had happened. Perhaps I should take the shoelaces out of *my* tennis shoes and put them in Bill's. Of course they would be too short, but maybe I could convince him that his laces had shrunk from getting wet in the rain. The only problem with that idea was we hadn't had any rain in Southern California for several months.

Another option was to take the laces out of another pair of Bill's shoes and put them in the sneakers. But that didn't seem like a workable idea because, although Bill doesn't have the greatest eye for fashion colors, I was pretty sure he would notice that his *white* tennis shoes suddenly sported *black* laces.

Under normal circumstances I would have just hopped in the car, driven to the drugstore, and bought a pack of new laces. But as I recovered from chemotherapy, the doctors had forbidden me to drive, so that option was out. At about that point in my scheming, I heard Bill coming through the house. "Have you seen my tennis shoes?" he asked.

Without a word, I handed them to him. He headed into the kitchen and sat down. I stood there waiting for the next question. It came in less than a second: "Where are the laces?"

I carried the pan into the kitchen and held it out to him. "Here," I said, trying to maintain some semblance of dignity.

He glanced into the shoelace sauce, then looked up at me. "What is this?" he asked.

"It's your shoelaces," I answered. "I soaked them overnight in bleach."

Bill looked again at the milky white gravy and heaved the same sigh I'd heard a million times when I'd burned yet another dinner entrée (back in the days when I was still cooking actual meals). "Oh, brother," he muttered, shaking his head solemnly.

I couldn't stand the pressure any longer. I burst out laughing as Bill left the room in indulgent disgust, his laceless tennis shoes flopping against his heels as he walked. I couldn't wait to call up my friends and share the funny story. "Oh, you'll never guess what happened to Bill's shoelaces," I told them, giggling right from the start. "I turned them into oatmeal!"

Oh, it felt so good to laugh that day—a day stuck in a week dotted with grueling medical procedures and stressful doctors' appointments—and share that laughter with my friends.

I've often thought, during the hard times in my life, that laughter is the language of hope. We cry. We moan. We pray for help. And because we hold on to hope, we are eventually able to laugh again, even in the dark places. We know that whatever the current problem is, it didn't come to stay. As the Bible says again and again, "It came to pass"! In my work with parents who have endured difficult crises with their children, I've been amazed to find that some of those who have been through the most pain seem to have the greatest capacity for joy. I read somewhere that sorrow hollows out our hearts so that God can fill them with love and joy. These pain-scarred but joy-filled parents are living examples of that bit of wisdom.

Our hope is God himself. He has promised to walk beside us no matter what difficulties we face here on earth—and to bring us home to heaven to live with him for eternity. Because we know our ultimate destination, because we're focusing on heaven, we can face the treacherous stretches of our lives' pathways with courage and strength. And we can maintain a "cheerful heart," one that's always ready to laugh when our shoelaces turn to mush.

~ *Dear Jesus, thank you for the healing, hope-filled gift of laughter. Help me be ready to seek it and share it wherever I go. Amen.*

The Ever-Moving Shadow

LUCI SWINDOLL

*My flesh and my heart may fail, but God is the strength
of my heart and my portion forever. (Psalm 73:26)*

*I*t never occurred to me to grow old. I've always thought
you're as young as you feel. But when I turned seventy in
the fall of 2002, my philosophy of life was tested. I'm happy
to say, so far so good. I'm not old yet, and to prove my point?
Well, the first trip I took after my seventieth birthday was an
excursion to Antarctica. That was the only continent on which
I had never set foot, and I was very eager to see it. On the first
of December, Mary Graham, Nicole Johnson, Andrea
Grossman, and I headed out for a fifteen-day trip to the bottom of the world.

There were many moments I look back on with tremendous pleasure—like giving a birthday party for Nicole, complete with gifts, balloons, fabulous toasts, much singing, and
an igloo-shaped cake with tiny marzipan penguins holding
the candles. That was a highlight. As was spending hours
drawing icebergs that were as large as Wal-Mart or as small as
a refrigerator. Or taking pictures of frolicking Orca whales.
Or making a snowman or snow angels on an ice floe as thick

as a five-story building. But the most wonderful memory is one that's so totally unique it will never be captured again even if I live to be one hundred. Or one thousand. It simply won't happen!

Monday afternoon, December 9, 2002, shortly after a kayaking class, the *M.S. Endeavour* docked at a place called Port Lockroy, a British postal station. The captain pulled the ship right up to an enormous iceberg and *parked*. Literally. Port Lockroy is in the middle of nowhere. I'm not kidding! Small groups of us went by Zodiac boats over to the station and climbed over rocks, ice, snow, and penguins to get up to the building, situated on a small bluff. Once we got inside, there were several rooms with memorabilia from the 1940s and '50s and a small post office where one could buy stamps, educational packs, T-shirts, and ball caps. (Of course, I bought everything.) The two people running the place were a British man who looked to be in his fifties and a young woman, who I supposed was his daughter, in her early twenties.

As I wandered around from room to room, checking out the place and snapping a few pictures, I wound up in a small area that had an old-fashioned record player and a few 33-rpm records. One of the folks in our party asked if the gentleman would play something on it. "Sure, I'd be delighted," he said in his lovely British brogue, and put on a song called "Umbrella Man," sung by two English guys, Flanagan and Allen. The minute the music started, I thought, *I know this song.* I had learned it as a child from my mother and hadn't sung it in sixty years. As soon as that old player snapped and crackled into music, I began to sing with all my heart, and to my utter surprise, as I was singing the Brit asked if I'd dance with him. I nodded "of course," and as I sang, we danced through the entire song.

Here I was in my red parka, earmuffs, gloves, life vest, and waterproof pants, with a camera slung around my neck, dancing and singing for all I was worth in a little post office in Antarctica. And, somehow, I remembered every single word of the song. It was one of the most spontaneous, serendipitous, enjoyable experiences I've ever had in my life.

And here's the capper: I could have so easily missed that moment. I could have thought it was too far or too risky to take such a trip in the first place. Or once I was there and experienced trouble walking on that uncertain terrain, I could have stayed on the ship and not disembarked at Port Lockroy. Or when I recognized the music, I could have kept my mouth shut and not sung. Or having been asked to dance, I could have said no, thank you. But because I chose to live fully in the moment, I have that memory for the rest of my life. No one can take it away. If I do live to be one hundred, I'll not remember that day without breaking into a smile.

The famous architect Frank Lloyd Wright once said, "The present is the ever-moving shadow that divides yesterday from tomorrow. In that lies hope." There is no doubt that aging is finally going to get the best of my body, but it doesn't have to get the best of my hope. I believe when we hope, we're ageless anyway. Hope enables us to share life's experiences with humor and compassion, accept what is, reflect without regret, and strive for what can be.

I may get out of breath when I dance and sing; I may walk

with a limp because of a bone spur; I may forget where I put my car keys; I may take longer naps in the afternoon or carry an extra piece of luggage for all my meds. But I'll tell you this: I wouldn't trade this age for anything. I spent all I had getting here and I'm happy to report it's worth the price. Besides, being this age doesn't mean I have to forfeit any of the ages I've already been. I've learned lots of things along the way that have given me perspective. I've learned how wonderful it is simply to enjoy reflection. To have the strength to handle challenges with wisdom and hope. To face life with the knowledge that God absolutely keeps his Word.

As each of us shares the mortality of life, we are constantly reminded that everything is temporary. We can't hang on to this life. It's going to be taken from us one way or another. So why not enjoy the ever-moving shadow that's on the horizon right now? It's the present. Live it. Love it. Hope in it.

Excuse me, I have to go now. There's a song and a dance in me just begging to get out.

~ *No matter how I feel today, Lord, give me victory and joy in you. Keep my eyes on you and the hope there is in trusting you. Don't let me get sidetracked by wishing I were younger or regretting anything about my current circumstances. This is the day you've given me. Help me live fully this very minute. Amen.*

Daily Brush Strokes

PATSY CLAIRMONT

~

Give us this day . . . (Matthew 6:11 NASB)

My friend Pat Wenger and I love to play with water-colors. It's not that we're especially good. Neither of us is dealing with a full color palette, but we're nervy. We often giggle at our colorful results, tilting our pictures in all directions trying to find an angle that might help others identify our mysterious offerings. Pat painted an orange once that looked just like a bagel while I dabbed away at a lily that took on the appearance of a mortified giraffe.

Recently Pat decided to try her brush at a beach scene with two young boys playing at the shoreline with their red plastic pails full of dreams. I thought it quite an ambitious project, especially with the history of our previous results. Yet the picture turned out amazingly well. The sun-drenched beach and white-capped water were visually pleasing and the children endearing. Pat and I decided it helps to paint what we love: sunny days filled with those most important to us.

Pat is the mom of three grown sons and a grandma of five, so she has a passion for boys, buckets, and beaches. She raised her sons near the ocean, so surfs and sailboats were a daily part of their landscape. And Pat was the kind of mom to join the boys in whatever they were doing. Her eyes ignite with glee when she speaks of her sons' childhood days. It's not that it was all easy; it never is. But there were more days of smooth sailing than of rough seas.

And isn't that true about our lives? When we count them up, more days are easy than chaotic, which gives us hope during hard times that eventually things will smooth out. Some rugged years tend to dim that truth in our churning minds, but if you're like me, when my head clears I remember the good ol' days when my toes were buried in the warm beach while the children built castles and feasted on sandy hot dogs.

I love conversations that begin with "Remember the time . . ." because more than likely we are going to reminisce about some fun-filled days.

I remember when we endured Michigan winters, which don't offer beaches, so on occasion when our boys would step off the school bus on a snowy Friday we would pile in the car and head for an affordable (cheap) hotel. Of course, we always chose one with an indoor pool where we could lollygag around the perimeter while the boys splashed about as though it were summer. Even the smell of chlorine inside and the icy display outside didn't diminish our family fun. We always took a pocket full of saved coins for the game room and then ate a lavish meal of hamburgers and fries to finish off the experience before braving the weather and sliding back home.

Hmm, I wonder how that event would look on canvas? Definitely not as appealing as the seashore, but it was what fit our options and it was a treat for us all. Actually, most of our smooth sailing days were made up of the routine things of life—like Southern fried chicken at Grandma's house, singing together in the car, church activities, playing Yahtzee, bowls of hot buttered popcorn, and jaunts to the Dairy Queen.

It's easy to underestimate the value of life's routines. We tend to want to escape the commonplace, yet routine gives predictability to our existence; it helps forge steady places. Also, it's often those day-to-day memories that bring us the warmest flood of emotions later.

When I think of my mom while I was growing up, I remember how sweet she always smelled, the particular care she took with the endless ironing, and how tidy she kept our home. I remember her thoughtfulness of trimming the crust off my sandwiches, the smell of baking powder biscuits wafting through the house, the sounds of her hymn singing while she cleaned, and her compassion toward hurting folks.

I'm not sure I could capture any of those things in my painting efforts. (After witnessing Pat's seaside success, I was inspired and tried a portrait of my grandson. Mysteriously he had the same giraffelike look as my lily.) So while my painting skills are minimal, my awareness of the hope infused in everyday living grows.

Here's my suggestion: Buy a tin of colors and paint a sailboat on a glassy sea to deepen your gratitude for smooth sailing days. I did, but it looked just like a mortified . . . well, never mind.

~ *Lord, when everything is going well, I sometimes forget what brush strokes of hope those days are to my life, to my emotions, and to my sanity. When my attempts to express myself fall miserably short, may my heart praise still be full of all the hues of gratitude. Thank you for the reminder of hope that comes when I look across the waters and spot the sailboat gliding seamlessly across the horizon. Amen.*

The Scandal Package

MARILYN MEBERG

But their trust should be in the living God,
who richly gives us all we need for our
enjoyment. (1 Timothy 6:17 NLT)

Mary Graham, president of Women of Faith, has incredible administrative skills and impeccable taste, and she has been a dear friend for over twenty years. Because I trust her, when she announced last spring that I needed to get an apartment in Dallas, I paused reflectively before saying, "Are you crazy? I don't even like Dallas!"

"That's not the point, Marilyn," she patiently explained. "With twenty-nine Women of Faith conferences scattered from the West Coast to the East Coast, you need to be in the middle of the country to reduce your flying time as well as energy output."

I thought about her suggestion as I left her in the Dallas airport and rushed to catch the one and only afternoon flight from Dallas to Palm Springs. Her parting words, "If you lived here, you'd be home now," rang in my ears.

The phone was ringing as I walked in the door of my darling little condo in Palm Desert. It was Mary. She had found a darling little apartment in Frisco, a suburb of Dallas. She and a couple of other friends (also Frisco residents) had set out immediately to find the perfect place for me. I began to feel hopeful for a less rigorous travel schedule. It had never occurred to me to hope for such a solution. But there it was, taking shape before my eyes and before my even asking.

I eagerly agreed to take the apartment. Mary signed the rental agreement on my behalf and scurried about to set up utilities as well as rental furniture to coordinate with my arrival date. Talk about smooth sailing; everything was falling into place perfectly.

As I was packing to take off for Dallas the following week, Mary called me. With what sounded like a stifled giggle, she reported an interesting development as she negotiated the furniture deal. Trying to keep the rental expense as manageable as possible, the furniture rep suggested Mary sign for what was called the "scandal package." That included everything one needed but could be returned the minute the furniture no longer served its purposes.

I pondered the implications of the scandal package. "Well, Mary, do I have to whip up an occasional scandal in order to keep the furniture? I'm not sure I'll have time for scandal . . . you could tell them I'm open to just a touch, but for the most part I'm pretty busy." They delivered the furniture.

As I expected, I loved the apartment as well as the scandal package furniture! An unexpected perk with the apartment is its location. It sits up from a little stream full of turtles that swim about, dive, resurface, and then beach on a small sand bar in the middle of the stream. I found myself constantly rushing to the window to watch them as well as count how many were "beaching." One morning I counted thirty-two black-shelled clumps all sunning themselves at the same time.

On that same morning I was drinking my tea, watching the turtles, and basically luxuriating in my good fortune when suddenly my attention became focused on a turtle couple engaging in mysterious behavior for which I had no category. *Mercy,* I thought, *am I witnessing a scandal outside my own window?*

I went back into the kitchen, poured another cup of tea, and was struck with the giggle-producing realization that the scandal package extends far beyond my couch, coffee table, dining room set, and queen-size bed. It's alive and well on the sand bar outside my apartment. I thought, *Well, the good thing is, at least the pressure for scandal is off of me now.*

At the end of last season, I bought the scandal package furniture and arranged to keep the apartment. My home away from home is my smooth-sailing gift from God. The location not only cuts down on travel time, but it's a little harbor to which I return after a busy weekend. God's Word says in James 1:17, "Whatever is good and perfect comes to us from God above" (NLT). I say, "Thank you, God—and thank you, Mary."

~ *Lord God, I thank you for the harbor you continually provide even when we don't know we need one. Your caring for the comfort and "enjoyment" of your children is astounding. Amen.*

All Day Long

SHEILA WALSH

*Show me your ways, O LORD, teach me your paths;
guide me in your truth and teach me, for you are God my
Savior, and my hope is in you all day long. (Psalm 25:4–5)*

I have never been much of a water drinker. I know that water is good for me. I know that our bodies are made up of bucketfuls of the stuff. I've read articles that assert that those who drink several glasses of water every day are thinner and have better skin than those of us who don't. And yet I remained unmoved.

Then I joined a weight-loss club after one particularly indulgent Christmas and was told that the success of the plan rested on one's commitment to drink eight glasses of water each and every day. I got up to leave before the guru of thin could trap me behind the water cooler.

"I think I can help you," she said.

"I know you do," I replied. "I can see it in your eyes."

"The thought of sitting down and consuming eight glasses of water is intimidating, I understand that," she continued. "What I recommend is that you start with one bottle and drink a little throughout the day. Every hour or so have a few sips. Do you think you would be willing to try that?"

"I could try," I replied, pathetically.

The next morning I stared at the large bottle of water on the kitchen table. I circled it a few times, then dived in and swallowed a couple of sips. After my shower I attacked it again. I had some with lunch and a bit more as I read a book. By the end of the day I was surprised to discover that the bottle was empty. I tried again the next day and the next. By the end of the week I was drinking two large bottles each day. It became part of my life, a new habit that was a discipline but one from which I knew I would reap great benefits.

I considered that concept in my relationship with Christ, the Living Water. It's easy for me to spend time with the Lord in the morning and then get so caught up in the busyness of my day that it's bedtime again and I realize it's been hours since I've taken in the life-giving water of hope he offers all day long.

"Show me your ways, O LORD, teach me your paths; guide me in your truth and teach me, for you are God my Savior, and my hope is in you all day long" (Psalm 25:4–5).

The psalmist's cry is to know the ways of God and to walk in those ways consistently, every moment of every day. Some commentaries suggest that this psalm may have been written after David's adulterous affair, so there is a renewed sense of a need for God's help each moment. By God's grace I have never found myself in that particular place, but I know that without God's help and hope I, too, will lose my way. I know that I need to partake of the Living Water all day long.

I have found all sorts of new ways to do that. I listen to worship tapes in my car and lift my voice in praise to God whether I feel like it or not. I choose a verse at the beginning of the day to chew on all day long. I have made a practice of noticing the world around me and thanking God for the beauty of his creation. I pray with my son as we drive to school in the morning, and I have my Bible with me in the car as I sit in the carpool line at the end of his day.

It's one thing to acknowledge that God is our only hope, but does the way we live our lives on a daily basis reflect that reality? All day long God longs for our company. All day long God longs to show mercy to us. All day long God loves to hear our needy hearts and fill our thirsty lives. Today, let's drink deeply of the one who is our hope all day long.

~ *Jesus, thank you that today and every day you long for my company. You are my hope and my life—my consistent nourishment whether the voyage is smooth or rough. Teach me to drink deeply of your living water all day long. Amen.*

He's Always There

NICOLE JOHNSON

Praise be to you, O LORD, God of our father Israel, from everlasting to everlasting. (1 Chronicles 29:10)

He drives a teal van, and in the mornings you can see it at the beach along Ocean Avenue. He parks in a metered space, which is free before 9 A.M., and he plays his electric guitar while staring out at the ocean.

I first noticed him one morning when I went running. I noticed him because he plays an electric guitar but it isn't plugged in to anything. He stands facing the sea, quietly playing an instrument designed to make a lot of noise. Every morning he is there. He is charming. I've never met him, but every time I go for a run, he is there. He's probably in his sixties, and he has gray hair. Sometimes he wears a ball cap. The strap on his guitar is purple, and I can't tell a lot about his face because he's always focused on the water. But the thing I notice most about him after two years of running is that he's always there.

I am not a consistent runner. Because of my travel, because of my knees, because of a lot of things, I'm not out there every morning. But he is. He is the picture of consistency. Sometimes when I don't go for a run, I look out my window down the beach to see if I can find the teal van. And I always do.

Something about his consistency speaks to me deeply. I have come to count on him in a small way. Day after day, he shows up. Rain or shine, fog or clear, warm or cold, he's there. I would add snow, but we don't have that in Santa Monica. I would be willing to bet that if we did, he'd be there in that too. He's far more dependable than the post office, whose hours I can't quite figure out. I could set my watch by him. When I'm five minutes into my run and I see his van and I see that purple strap slung over his shoulder, somehow all seems right with the world.

So what is it about consistency that means so much to us? It gives us hope. It gives the universe a sense of order and purpose. Most of us don't even realize we hunger for such things until we taste them and find them so satisfying. We have a deep longing for things to be consistent and true. We feel this yearning when we experience it in some small way.

I respect and appreciate that man for something he has no idea he's doing: He is just being himself, with no idea that a runner in the park counts on him like the sunrise. He may be in a terrible marriage and just want to get out of the house every morning. He may be a lifelong single or homeless and mad at the world, but I doubt it. Anger and bitterness tend to make us break our commitments, not get better at them. He's remarkable to me, and I'm guessing he knows the one who made the ocean he's so in love with, because every morning he goes out and plays his music.

I once heard a motivational speaker say, "If you can't be

good, be there." I wasn't sure that I agreed with his statement when I first heard it, but I think I do now. Not everybody can be a world-class musician on the electric guitar. But there is something very right about just showing up day after day and giving what you've got. Unapologetically. He isn't trying to impress anyone. His consistency isn't to prove a point. He is just a man who makes time every morning to serenade the ocean. And just by showing up, he serenades my soul and reminds me of my Savior.

Creator God, maker of land and sea, give us a heart to show up every day and play our songs for you. Grant us peace as we realize we don't always have to "be good"; sometimes we can just "be there." Let us worship you with our unplugged hearts and be captivated by the steady surf of your everlasting love. Amen.

PART THREE

Stormy Weather Ahead

I Remember . . .

MARILYN MEBERG

*I recall all you have done, O LORD; I remember
your wonderful deeds of long ago. (Psalm 77:11 NLT)*

Why do we often lose hope in stormy weather? Why do we sometimes feel we won't survive the gales lashing at us with such fury? For one thing, we're human. Isaiah 2:22 says that humans "are as frail as breath" (NLT). Knowing our frailty and knowing our tendency to lose hope, let me share with you a storm-survival method I've used since childhood. I didn't know it was a scriptural method until I became an adult. But it has given me much hope as I have lived out my "frail-as-breath" days.

The suggestion for surviving storms and maintaining hope is found in Psalm 77:11. Quite simply, it is to *remember* all the times God has come through for us. When we think back on God's faithfulness, then we can rest in hope.

I first put that together as a method when I was five years old and living in Chino, California. I can't imagine it now, but I had a fascination with snakes. They appeared so helplessly peculiar; no arms, no legs, and yet they could zip along with amazing speed if I went after one. Fascinating. There was a lot of building going on around our little house, which seemed to unsettle the snake population. Many came into our yard to find peace. The only deterrent to peace was the little girl (me) who lived there and who liked to get up close and personal. "Unattractive child," they all hissed as they quickly slithered away, hoping to leave me in the dust.

One morning I was snake stalking but with little success. There seemed to be no activity behind the bushes or vines. Thinking I might try some other pastime, I was suddenly stopped in my tracks. Directly in front of me was a snake coiled up like a garden hose. All the snakes I stalked hotfooted it away from me. This one seemed to be waiting. It not only seemed to be waiting; it made little castanet sounds. I'd never seen or heard anything like it. Fascinating.

I was about to hunker down for a closer inspection when my mother tore out of the house and snatched me. The snake lunged with lightning speed . . . it missed . . . we slowly backed into the house while it resumed its coil and wild castaneting. It was then I learned the difference between California king snakes and rattlesnakes. I gave up snake stalking. There was no doubt in my child mind that God had saved me from certain death. (I tended to be a bit theatrical.)

Five years later I was riding my bike down the milelong road leading to our Lonely Acres home. The paper and mail were safely tucked in my basket. My dog, King, who'd been trotting along ahead of me, stopped abruptly and began barking ferociously. His fur was literally standing on end. Curious, I put my bike down and walked slowly into the dense undergrowth.

Then it was my turn for spiked hair. Sitting awkwardly on a log, munching huckleberries, was an enormous bear. He appeared to be absorbed in his huckleberry snack and may not even have seen me, but I was taking no chances. I took off like an MD-80, leaving my bike and dog in the road. I didn't know the bear was not lumbering along behind me until I burst breathlessly into the kitchen. I had a sense my parents questioned whether I had actually seen a bear. However, the next day a neighboring farmer reported seeing a "huge" grizzly in his woods. Uh-huh! Another "remembrance" was tucked away; God saved me again.

I gathered a number of other memory trophies as I grew up, but with increased maturity as well as experience I learned that sometimes the storm continued to lash at me even when I prayed, asked for deliverance, and remembered. As an only child I feared my parents would die and I'd grow up in an orphanage. Images of Oliver Twist begging for one more bowl of gruel accompanied my fear images. They did not die, I grew up, and "more gruel" was never an issue. Nevertheless, my parents and I were a warm, self-sustaining unit and I dreaded the day when they would inevitably be called home. My mother was my spiritual rock, mentor, and priest. She was gentle, refined, intellectual, and deeply appreciative of my zany nature. She was everything I wanted to be. She told me I was everything she would have liked to be. Since I barely passed algebra and never understood the intricacies of my home economics sewing machine, I was highly flattered by her admiration.

In 1987 my mother died as a result of a number of medical challenges: unsuccessful brain surgery and subsequent pneumonia. I remember sitting in the parking lot of the hospital and looking up at Mom's hospital room, where I'd spent the last several days. I couldn't turn the key to start my car. I knew when I came back it would be to make funeral arrangements.

"Lord Jesus, I can't let her go," I prayed. I remembered the times she had survived several other health crises, and I begged God to meet her yet again, to sustain her, to heal her. The storm in my heart raged. She died the next morning.

Was God indifferent? Did he turn a deaf ear to my prayers? No. God is never indifferent to our pain, nor does he ignore the prayers of his children. But I was reminded yet again about where to place my hope. God promises always to calm the storm. He calmed my storm by reminding me that each life has an ordained termination point. It was time for Mom to go home. It was also time for me to release her.

God brought me safely into the harbor of his never-failing presence and his sovereign love for me when my circumstances hurt. He did that for me; I want always to remember.

~ *Lord God, thank you for strengthening your "frail-as-breath" child. Amen.*

Gravitating toward Hope

LUCI SWINDOLL

~

Now faith is being sure of what we hope for and certain of what we do not see. (Hebrews 11:1)

No matter how you slice it, nobody wants to be in a hospital. Even with the best of care, attentive nurses, and around-the-clock attention, all one thinks of is *going home*. This was my case during a three-day stay in a Sacramento hospital last spring. I longed for a doctor (any doctor) to come into my room and say, "You look great; get outta here"—or something to that effect.

After being whisked by ambulance to the hospital on a Saturday night, I was diagnosed with atrial fibrillation. In layman's terms, this is where the atrium (top part of the heart) twitches and palpitates faster than the ventricle (bottom part of the heart). After two full days of undergoing numerous tests, having my vitals checked regularly, my heart monitored consistently, my blood taken routinely, and my mind probed for information I considered both personal and private, a lovely, tall woman came into my darkened room at 1:00 A.M. and introduced herself. "Good morning," she said sweetly. "I'm Doctor Golden."

"Good morning. Nice to see you," I said, although I couldn't see very well at that hour.

She listened to my heart as she whispered, "Good . . . Excellent . . . Fantastic."

Obviously, she was very pleased about something, which certainly wasn't my hairstyle or hospital gown.

"Your heart no longer has atrial fibrillation, Luci. At some point it healed itself," she said, smiling. "That's good news. And if you can sustain this sinus rhythm, I'll spring you today."

I had no idea what "sinus rhythm" meant, but even in my predawn, groggy state I was sure of two things: I hadn't healed myself, and I knew exactly what "spring you today" meant. I was going home if I did something right—like keeping the beat while I blew my nose. That Golden apparition appeared just long enough to give me solid hope, then vanished into the hallway. What a wonderful moment.

I learned later that "sinus rhythm" is when your heart contracts in a coordinated fashion. We have a natural pacemaker called the sinus node, which God put there so the intricate timing system of the heart does what it should. (I *loved* learning that term and am now looking for ways to use it all the time). But here's the best part of knowing this: Sinus rhythm has nothing to do with me or my will, my plans, or how I blow my nose. I have no power over my own heartbeat. Only God controls that. My heart, and my life, is in his hands. And so is my complete confidence.

As I lay in the darkness of that hospital room, I knew exactly what I hoped for. I wanted to get out of the hospital!

And with that in mind I believed God would bring it about. I prayed quietly that he would keep my heart rate slow and steady.

Dr. Norman Cousins says, "The human body experiences a powerful gravitational pull in the direction of hope. That is why the patient's hopes are the physician's secret weapon. They are the hidden ingredients in any prescription."

When we're in situations where our health is on the line, we can do nothing more than trust. We're not in charge of the rhythms of our bodies. God is. We can't change the beat of our hearts. God can. We don't know what will happen to us physically. God does. Nonetheless, when we experience a pull in the direction of hope, I believe it enhances our healing capacity. Even though treatment comes from without, our health comes from within. My hope, and the hope of my friends, was a powerful force during those few days. Hope was a buoy to my spirit and a balm to my soul.

After the hospitalization, my own doctor studied me like a book and concluded that I'm in very good health. My heart continues to stay in "sinus rhythm," and I thank God. I'm more aware than ever, though, that he is in control—and I trust that.

There's an interesting phenomenon about health. We pay little attention to it when it's good. We generally recover easily from illness. Ordinary stress might annoy us but doesn't make our blood pressure rise. Sleep is restful and aging gradual. All systems are in working order. We go along either giving our health no thought at all or assuming we'll have boundless energy and eternal happiness in an ageless body forever. I've spent a lot of my life this way. It's easy to take good health for granted.

However, since I've had this little heart episode, I've been acutely aware that every day I'm well, energetic, and in functioning order is an enormous gift. I can't heal myself, but I can emphasize prevention. I can't stop the changes of time, but I can gravitate toward hope. I can't keep my heart in sinus rhythm, but I can trust God to take care of me no matter what.

This is good enough for me. It puts a spring in my step, and that spring is a river of life.

~ *Thank you, Lord, for the gift of life and health—for the rhythmic beat of my own heart. Enable me today to have faith, to live in peace and in the joy of your presence. And when life seems fragile and fleeting, remind me that my hope is in you. Amen.*

Heavenly Healing

BARBARA JOHNSON

*Our present troubles are quite small and won't last
very long. Yet they produce for us an immeasurably great
glory that will last forever! (2 Corinthians 4:17 NLT)*

When you've lived awhile with a life-threatening illness, taking down the old year's calendar and putting up the next one becomes a special ritual. Last December as I was setting about that task, I marveled that there had been several times during the previous months when I hadn't thought I would make it through my battle with cancer to see another year. And there also had been times when I wished I wouldn't! But there I was, the week after Christmas, hanging another new calendar on the wall and wondering what those next twelve months would bring.

A few weeks earlier, as I had prepared the December issue of our Spatula Ministries newsletter, I had asked my doctor what I should tell all the friends and supporters who write and call to ask about my health. He is a dear friend who has taken care of me for years, long before cancer required that I adopt oncology specialists and brain surgeons into my medical "family." He smiled and nodded, probably reviewing mentally the medical adventures I had endured the previous year. Finally, he said, "Tell them you're making a hellish recovery!"

I tossed that phrase around in my head for a while and decided it did, indeed, describe my situation. I was recovering, but some of the procedures and problems I had endured to reach that state had been truly hellish. Still, I thought the phrase lacked something; it didn't express my condition fully. Finally, I realized the thing that was missing was *hope*. The phrase didn't reflect the optimism and faith that had kept my spirits up even as my health had at times wavered. So when I wrote about the doctor's words in our newsletter, I told the readers my "hellish recovery" was becoming "heavenly healing." That assessment seemed more in line with the hope I cling to day and night.

The apostle Paul's reminder in 2 Corinthians 4:17 is very real to me because I've already seen it come true in several earthly ways. After two of our sons were killed and a third disappeared into the homosexual lifestyle, I spent a year in my bedroom counting the roses on the wallpaper. Finally, in desperation, I got in my car and drove to a high viaduct, planning to step on the gas, drive the car over the edge, and end it all. But something held me back. That something was *hope*. From the farthest dark corner of my mind, God's promises came trickling back to me, and instead of giving up on life, I gave up to God. I prayed the two-word prayer of relinquishment: "Whatever, Lord!" I put my hand in God's and set off with him to face whatever came next.

Looking back, I see that the years since then have been

another kind of hellish recovery that has led me to heavenly healing. It's hard to think of the death of two sons and the long estrangement of a third son as "present troubles" that are "quite small," as Paul said. Even now there are days when a special memory of Steve or Tim may float through my mind and reduce me to tears in an instant. But the tears don't last long, because in that same moment I'm reminded of the "immeasurably great glory" that's ahead of me. Someday I'm going to see my boys again, and that joy "will last forever!"

Meanwhile, I focus on heavenly healing of the old hurts that once plagued my life—and not just on my own healing, but on helping others find healing too. I wake up in the morning and pray, "Okay, Lord, I give you this day. Whatever it brings, I dedicate it to you." Then the phone will ring or a letter will arrive. Often the first words are, "You don't know me, but . . ." How touching it is to think that a stranger is reaching out to me to give them hope. These writers and callers know I've been through some very difficult challenges, and they're hoping I can help them find their way back to normalcy—or as normal as they can be when their hearts have been ripped to shreds. Usually the cries for help come from other moms who have been broadsided by some kind of missile of misery involving their children. One of them told me, "I know the view from that viaduct, Barb. In my broken heart, that's where I am right now."

What an honor to think I might offer these hurting parents a bit of encouragement and give them some hope to cling to when sorrow seems ready to swallow them up. That's where Paul's promise comes true for me in earthly ways. It's the boomerang principle at work. My experience with a harsh variety of "present troubles" gives me credentials to reach out to others who are just now entering the most challenging rapids of their own rivers of anguish. By helping them through the hellish recovery phase, I can join them in celebrating heavenly healing as their misery is replaced by hope. And that process brings me "immeasurably great glory" here on earth— glory that will propel me through my own future floods when they inevitably occur.

~ *Father, just as you have lifted me out of the raging waters so many times in the past, I long to be your lifeline to others who find themselves caught in terrifying eddies. Use me, Lord, in sickness and in health, to make the way easier for someone who is struggling. Amen.*

Yahoo!

SHEILA WALSH

~

Praise be to the God and Father of our Lord Jesus Christ!
In his great mercy he has given us new birth into a living
hope through the resurrection of Jesus Christ from the dead,
and into an inheritance that can never perish, spoil or fade—
kept in heaven for you, who through faith are shielded by
God's power until the coming of the salvation that is
ready to be revealed in the last time. (1 Peter 1:3–5)

Dad said I could do it," my son proclaimed as the sun kissed his blond, sand-filled hair.

"I'm sure Dad was kidding," I replied.

"He wasn't kidding. He's paying for it now," Christian said, pointing to a small kiosk on the boardwalk.

I looked up and saw Barry walking back to where we sat on the beach. In his hands he had two life vests.

"Are you nuts?" I inquired as soon as he was within hearing range.

"This will be fun," he said. "The guy said that kids as young as four can do it."

"That must be families with many, many kids and sunstroke," I suggested.

Ignoring my unlikely scenario, Barry and Christian suited up in their life vests and headed off to the ocean's edge. I followed right behind. The jet ski instructor began to give them a basic first lesson.

"What if they fall off?" I interrupted.

"That's what the life vests are for," he replied, continuing with his little speech.

"What about sharks?" I continued.

"We don't have sharks here," he said.

"What about jellyfish or big eels—or what about hurricanes that blow up out of nowhere consuming unsuspecting tourists?"

He didn't even answer that one.

"Just one more question," I begged. "Just tell me what the worst is that could happen."

He looked at Barry with great sympathy. "The worst that could happen is that they fall off and float in the water for a few moments. I think they could handle that, don't you?"

I watched as my husband and six-year-old child climbed on a jet ski together and took off across the waves. The faint sound of *yahoos!* floated back to me. Christian told me later that night as he sat in his bath that he had been afraid at first, but he'd so wanted to try it. "I decided just to go for it, Mom," he said with all the conviction of a true knight.

Once he was fast asleep, I thought about our day and the different ways that my son and I had handled our fear. His fear became a wind behind his back; mine, a pin in the balloon of possibility.

I may never be a jet skier, but I learned a valuable lesson

that day. As we face each new day in our journey with Christ, all sorts of things could happen; they might never happen, but they are possibilities. We could have a smooth-as-glass ride. Or severe winds could threaten our craft with the ring of the telephone or the simple act of opening a letter. Waves of circumstance could appear all-consuming.

So what do we know for sure?

Peter reminds us that because of God's great mercy we have a new reality. We are reborn into "a living hope" because of Christ's death and resurrection. We have an inheritance that can never perish, spoil, or fade—kept in heaven for us. It doesn't get any safer than that! Through faith we are shielded by God's power until the end of the age.

We need to hold on to the truth of God's Word every day, for it will be an anchor in a storm and a life vest if we do end up in the water for a while. When we face the worst that could happen in our voyage, we can enjoy the ride, because our hope is a living hope.

I asked Christian about the *yahoos!* the next day.

"I guess that's when you were having the most fun," I said.

"No, Mom, that's when I was afraid. I just yelled it anyway."

As you set sail today, the sea may be smooth as glass. If the wind kicks up, however, just lift your head and your heart to heaven and yell a faith-filled *yahoo!*

⌒ *Father, thank you that you are with me on this voyage. Thank you that in you I have a living hope, preserved for all eternity. Amen.*

Hope Hops!

LUCI SWINDOLL

~

But as for me, I will always have hope;
I will praise you more and more. (Psalm 71:14)

There's something wonderful about wisdom coming out of the mouth of a child.

My five-year-old friend Beverly is the proud owner of a tiny bunny rabbit her parents gave her for Easter. Beverly named the rabbit "Hope." She eagerly told me all the things they did together. Hope eats out of Beverly's hand and stays in a little bed at night right next to Beverly's. "Hope twitches her nose when you put a carrot in front of her." "Hope lifts her leg and scratches her ear." But best of all, "Hope hops!" Beverly told me. "She can even hop down the stairs and across the room." I was impressed.

It's a truth I learned long ago: Hope *does* hop. It moves from place to place, showing up just when we need it most. And you cannot keep it down. Just when you wonder if it's gone, it pops up out of nowhere as a wonderful surprise.

In Lamentations 3:19–23, we read of a time of affliction and bitterness that was displaced by remembering the hope that's in God's love and compassion. Romans 4:18 says

Abraham experienced hope against hope by believing God would make him the father of many nations even though his wife was long past her childbearing years. The Lord's delight is a product of those who put their hope in his unfailing love, says Psalm 147:11. Endurance is inspired by hope in the Lord Jesus in 1 Thessalonians 1:3. Hope hops throughout the pages of Scripture, assuring us it's still there. No matter what.

Hope hops all over the map . . . all over the Bible . . . all the time. No matter what the weather, the circumstances, or the odds.

It does the same in our lives. This isn't some outdated biblical concept, an anomaly that shows up at weird times if we keep all the rules and behave ourselves. No! Hope is ours for the taking every single minute. It's the assurance that things will make sense when there's no sense to make of things. How often I have said to myself, "Why, this makes no sense at all," or "It's just stupid to believe this way." Yet time and again I find myself hopeful; I just can't shake it. Hope hops into my mind and fights for me to be strong and of good courage.

I think of our dear friend Barbara Johnson and the battle she faced when the doctor told her she had a malignant brain tumor that required very delicate surgery. Immediately hope hopped into her heart. After the surgery, Barbara was asked if she had been afraid. "No," she said, "I had no fear. I knew the Lord was with me and all my friends and family were praying for me." That kind of hope is what has gotten her through the stormy times. It hasn't been easy, and there are times when Barbara must feel overwhelmed with emotions—a natural reaction for anyone facing something of that magnitude. But the hope Barbara has in Christ and what he promises about being with us in our pain, confusion, and sadness is what sees her through the worst of times. Each time we talk to her, she's hopeful. Irrepressible hope keeps her up and kickin' . . . planning the next thing. Never giving up.

I also love to hear Dayna Curry and Heather Mercer talk about their incarceration by the Taliban in Afghanistan for 107 days. Hope hopped into that prison with them, and if you've read their book or heard them speak, you know that their being there seemed to make no sense and the outlook for deliverance looked bleak. Yet they never abandoned hope. And hope never abandoned them.

My older brother, Orville, was a missionary in Argentina for thirty-six years. He's told me of times he and his family were down to their last dime or last grain of rice . . . and hope hopped through the door in the form of a friend, a gift, or a miracle to meet the need.

Hope hops.

Think of your own life. Can you remember when your circumstances made no sense? You did what you thought was right and things turned out badly. Maybe you invested in something that seemed like a sure reward, but your partner skipped off with the funds and now here you are with no capital, no companion, and no consolation. You gave your kids the best years of your life, but there's no gratitude from them and no desire in their hearts to follow the path of righteousness.

Don't abandon hope! It's full of surprises. It's a bunny rabbit, just waiting to hop on the scene and bring you a brighter day. All you need to do is find the door to the cage. It's inside you. Open it wide and let hope hop.

⌒ *Give me the courage, Lord, to believe you are providing a way of deliverance, even when the storm clouds are closing in. Remind me that you will never abandon me or leave me hopeless. Amen.*

Storm Savvy

PATSY CLAIRMONT

~

Be prepared in season and out of season.
(2 Timothy 4:2)

My husband awoke this morning in the wee hours to find me crawling around on the bedroom floor in the dark. Undaunted, he quipped, "Fall out of bed?"

"Nope, I lost my glasses," I answered. "I put them on the bedstand last night and now I can't find them. I think I must have knocked them off in my sleep." With that admission he joined me (sweet man) in the search.

Some husbands might have found that middle-of-the-night crawling behavior a dark cloud on the horizon of their wife's sanity. My hubby, after forty years of living with me, found it the norm.

Early warning signs can be important information whether we are talking about a wacky woman's mental dexterity, threatening health issues, or impending storms.

Red at night, sailors delight. Red in the morning, sailors take warning.

That old weather ditty was an alert for sailors about the importance of keeping an eye to the sky for storm warnings.

Once they spotted a magenta sunrise, they could take necessary precautions—you know, like stay on shore and stock the galley.

I think that's what Old Testament Abigail did, because when the weather siren screeched in her neighborhood, she hurried to face the crisis. Scripture tells us she was married to a rich fool. (Definitely not the type of fellow who would help his wife find her lost eyeglasses.) Even his name, Nabal, meant folly. He was considered evil while Abigail was said to be intelligent and beautiful. When Nabal foolishly insulted David by his unwillingness to pay his soldiers with a food offering, David vowed to murder all the men in Nabal's camp. When Abigail heard the thunder of David's men on the horizon, she headed for the pantry. There she pulled from the shelves bread, figs, wine, and roasted grain, as well as five prepared sheep. Her pantry was brimming with supplies. Abigail was ready for the storm troopers.

I wonder if being married to an angry man put Abigail on constant storm alert. It usually doesn't take long for a fool to show his magenta disposition. And because Nabal was greedy in his dealings, I'm sure Abigail had run interference between him and others before. She probably had become fairly aerobic putting out Nabal's fires. One thing we know for sure is that Abigail kept her shelves well stocked. Why, even on a good day, if you stopped by my house, you would not find five sheep already prepared.

Imagine if, when Abigail heard that David's armed men were on their way, she had to make a run to Kroger for food. By the time she parked her camel, stood in line at the Palm Frond Bakery, and hotfooted it home, Nabal and the workers would have been history. Fortunately, she was ready to serve up food to satisfy the rumblings of a hostile army. But foodstuffs were not all that Abigail had been storing up for a rainy day. It was obvious that from her internal storehouse she pulled from the shelves faith, integrity, hope, and courage. Now those aren't items you can find at the store, borrow a cup of from your neighbor, or purchase at a discount. Those qualities come from a history of turning to the Lord during threatening weather, following his directions even as bolts of lightning rip through the sky, and resting in his plan amid pelting rain.

How do we know Abigail had those qualities? Well, instead of calling her maidens and heading for a storm shelter to save her own life, she went down alone to meet David and his four hundred scary men (very different scenario than Robin Hood and his Merry Men). Men who came angry, armed, and famished. I don't believe that kind of courage suddenly appears on empty shelves; rather, it is built inside a human heart through a history of storing up trust in God. Abigail's concern for the lives of her people was a greater priority to her than easing her own fears, and when David approached she bowed to the ground. Her words to David are amazing: "On me alone, my lord, be the blame" (1 Samuel 25:24 NASB).

Hello, Abigail! What are you saying? These men have come to kill the person responsible for your household's lack of hospitality. Initially I thought her approach ludicrous, but then I looked at the results, which left me breathless and pondering. I wonder if it wasn't startling and refreshing to David to have someone take responsibility for a wrongdoing instead of blaming everyone else. Abigail then followed her statement with a request to speak and to be heard, which was granted. By the time she finished, David's response was the opposite of his original intention: "Blessed be the LORD God of Israel, who sent you this day to meet me, and blessed be your discernment, and blessed be you, who have kept me this day from bloodshed, and from avenging myself by my own hand" (1 Samuel 25:32–33 NASB).

One woman's influence was powerful because she was not paralyzed by the anger of others but instead was storm savvy.

Hark! Is that a rumbling in the distance? Talk to you later—I'm heading for Kroger. I'm short on sheep.

(By the way, my hubby and I found my eyeglasses inside the bedcovers. Now if I could just stop making a spectacle of myself.)

~ *Lord, help us to be faithful and responsible in the little squalls of life so we have what it takes when the thunderclouds strike. Thank you for being God over all our storms. Amen.*

Keeping the Boat Afloat

MARILYN MEBERG

～

Submit to one another out of reverence
for Christ. (Ephesians 5:21)

I grew up thinking I didn't want to marry. Oddly enough, I was engaged at nineteen, and the plan was to marry two years later, after college graduation.

When Ken Meberg gave me my engagement ring on Thanksgiving Day, witnessed by our two families, I was immediately nauseous. The one thought that stabilized my insides that day was the fact that I had two years before the wedding.

During those two years I broke the engagement twice, postponed the wedding date once, and lost twenty pounds. Finally, on June 17, 1961, with the aid of a couple of tranquilizers, I marched resolutely down that church aisle where my father waited to perform the wedding ceremony and Ken marveled that I'd actually shown up.

The obvious question is, With all that apprehension, why did I go ahead with the marriage? Quite simply, I loved Ken. I figured if I was going to marry someone, I wanted to marry him. We had tons of fun, and he had a great family and was exceedingly bright, a Christian, and cute. It made sense to marry him. But my problem wasn't with Ken; it was with marriage. I feared losing my independence—no longer being mistress of my own domain. I feared I'd have a new captain come on board and I'd be subject to his chain of command.

But guess what I discovered! Ken wasn't into chain of command; he was committed to equality. We established and lived for thirty years in a partnership, not a dictatorship. I guess I hadn't recognized his style before we married. I think I believed that the minute I said, "I do," it would become, "You do."

What was the source of that fear? My dad was not a dictator, but he could be an inflexible leader at times. His say was the final say, and had I been married to him, I'd have had a number of things to say about his say. My mother did say a few things but for the most part was acquiescent. I was doubtful I could pull it off as well as she.

Is a successful marriage based on female acquiescence in the face of one-sided male dominance? I think not. In fact, those views can threaten smooth marital sailing and head a couple into stormy weather. Stormy weather inspires statements like, "Marriage is a bed of roses; most of them have thorns." Or "Marriage is the first step toward divorce."

We know Scripture tells us that marriage was instituted by God, and not just for the purpose of procreation. God said it isn't good for man to be alone. Eve was created to be a soul mate and companion for Adam. God puts a high premium on interrelatedness; he wanted Eve to share the fulfillment of mutuality in relationship. They were to be of one mind, body, and soul. That experience was lost with the disobedience in the Garden and the entrance of sin. From that point on, marriage lost its sinless mutuality of love and respect, and to marry, for some, has become to lie down in a bed of thorns.

Is marriage then a hopeless voyage doomed to repeated storms that threaten to capsize the ship? Absolutely not, but we need to see the relationship as God meant it to be. Genesis 3:16 predicted that one of the effects of the advent of sin would be a misuse of male power. "He shall rule over you" is not God's decree for relationship; it is a prediction of sin's effects on the human race. Scripture predicts that those with power will use it to exploit and abuse those with less power. This sin consequence is evident in international relationships, marital relationships, and even playground relationships. According to that system, power rules.

God sets an example of a better way. The entire Gospel of John shares how the Father respects, honors, and loves his Son. Jesus returns that respect, honor, and love. For example, the Father granted to the Son authority and power. Why? They were, and continue to be, united in purpose. They worked together as equals. Yet the Son did not make decisions without talking to the Father. He talked to the Father not because he was subordinate, but because he wanted to maintain continual communication with the Father.

I find this a very compelling example of how to love without the use of force or the flaunting of authority. When a husband shows his wife those tender considerations, it's very likely the wife will respond in like manner. I know I did.

Jesus also gives us an example of how women are to be honored. He risked the anger of the Jewish community by allowing a sinful woman to touch him. He also initiated a respectful dialogue with a social outcast, the Samaritan woman at the well. He chose women to be the first witnesses of his resurrection, invited women to travel with him, and gladly taught truth to women who sought his company.

Jesus did this in a Palestinian Jewish culture where women were not to go out in public, give testimony in court, inherit their husband's property, or be formally educated. In fact, the birth of a daughter was considered a loss. The example of Jesus alters some traditional understandings of male leadership. The challenge is to recognize that male leadership is not about maintaining power but about giving women greater honor, as Jesus did. "And you husbands must love your wives with the same love Christ showed the church. He gave up his life for her" (Ephesians 5:25 NLT).

To love as Jesus loves is a tall order for us fallible human beings. But I don't know any woman who could resist that kind of strong tenderness. That style of loving would have been all the assurance I needed to toss my tranquilizers and race down the aisle toward my groom.

〜 *Lord, it is mutual yieldedness that keeps a marital boat afloat. Enable us to do our part. Amen.*

The Drake Passage

NICOLE JOHNSON

Some of you set sail in big ships;
you put to sea to do business in faraway ports.
Out at sea you saw GOD in action,
saw his breathtaking ways with the ocean:
With a word he called up the wind—
an ocean storm, towering waves!
You shot high in the sky, then the bottom dropped out;
your hearts were stuck in your throats.
You were spun like a top, you reeled like a drunk,
you didn't know which end was up.
(Psalm 107:23–27 MSG)

A woman might read the passage above and think that the Bible is full of outdated metaphors she cannot relate to. After all, when was the last time she was out on the open sea with her heart in her throat?

This is the beauty of a metaphor. When someone writes the physical description of what he or she is going through, somehow we are set free to find a deeper truth of life that runs underneath a mere physical application. This is how we discover spiritual truth. We can find the meaning in our lives today, even if we've never been out on that kind of water.

But last year I really was in that kind of water. I was on a ship in thirty-foot swells, and I came face to face with the biblical accuracy in this passage! I happened to be taking a trip to Antarctica with Luci Swindoll and Mary Graham. We were warned ahead of time about the Drake Passage. This is an area of sea between Antarctica and South America where the Atlantic Ocean and the Pacific Ocean meet. The latitudes through there are not called the "roaring forties" for the way people dress!

This is rough water, folks. You can't walk about, and you can't eat. You'd better hold on to something, or you will be toppling over. There are ropes all over the ship and down the hallways just to keep you from falling down or running into the walls. In spite of this, you have bumps and bruises from all the tossing. You can't lie down or walk around to escape the pitching of the ship. You are rolling and reeling, and everything that isn't bolted down becomes a potential threat to your survival.

Although I had never been in such rough water physically, I hve been there emotionally. Many of you have too. The bottom drops out, your heart is stuck in your throat, and you are spinning and reeling. Someone said something that cut you to the very heart. You found out some information that knocked you onto the floor. You got a letter out of the blue that sent you pitching toward the water. The list of how it happens is long because our circumstances are so varied, but rough water is terrifying regardless of how we got there. Everything is upside down and you really don't know which end is up. Nothing is where it's supposed to be; nothing is where it was five minutes before.

On that trip I actually experienced on the sea what before I had experienced only in my spirit. And I decided to take the same approach in my distress:

> You called out to GOD in your desperate condition;
>> he got you out in the nick of time.
> He quieted the wind down to a whisper,
>> put a muzzle on all the big waves.
> And you were so glad when the storm died down,
>> and he led you safely back to harbor.
> So thank GOD for his marvelous love,
>> for his miracle mercy to the children he loves.
>> (Psalm 107:28–31 MSG)

Luci and I prayed many times in the midst of the rough Drake Passage. Our dear friend Mary was very sick and couldn't leave her bed. We cried out to God on her behalf and for ourselves. It was a very hard two and a half days. I cannot adequately express the joy we felt when the wind quieted down to a whisper, as God put a muzzle on all the big waves. There was much gladness aboard our vessel when the storm finally died down. And honestly, the next morning when we pulled slowly into the dock at the southernmost tip of South America, we all thanked God for his marvelous love and his miracle mercy.

Somehow, having survived the physical reality of crossing some of the roughest water in the world, my spirit knows there will be safe passage through more emotionally rough waters that inevitably lie ahead. Not without pitching and reeling and bumps and bruises. But my heart rests in the hope that God will sustain me through the roaring forties of my life just as he did through the rough latitudes of my trip.

〜 *Father, those of us in rough water cry out to you. Please put a muzzle on the waves beating against our vessels. Calm the raging seas around us. Remind us in the middle of the Drake Passages of our lives that this too shall pass and you will lead us safely back to the harbor. Help us to hang on tight to your marvelous love and your miracle mercy. Amen.*

Through All Our Storms

THELMA WELLS

~

All the days of my hard service I will
wait for my renewal to come. (Job 14:14)

alk about being in a storm . . . I just finished reading
Job's story again in the Bible. I had forgotten some of
the overwhelming waves of horror that brother experienced in
his life. And it seemed so unfair. At one time he was a very
wealthy man, kind of like Bill Gates or somebody like that. He
had lots of kids, including sons. During that time, if a man had
sons, he was the cat's meow. Obviously Job had a wife, too, and
they all enjoyed the luxury of many, many servants.

In those days, if a person was prosperous, he was considered righteous and blessed by God. If a person was not prosperous, he was thought of as being unrighteous and cursed by
God. Well, of course Job was viewed as being better than
blessed, thank you very much. His life was as smooth as a tub-
ful of warm bathwater.

But there were storm clouds on the horizon. God and
Satan had an interesting conversation in which God asked
Satan what he was up to (as if God didn't know). Satan told
God he was just roaming around on earth trying to find

somebody he could trip up. God asked Satan if he had considered his servant Job. Now that messed up my mind when I read it, because I thought, *How can God give up one of his children to that no-good devil?* But, of course, I had to repent right then and there. *Thelma, don't you know God knows what he's doing? He never makes a mistake. Ask God to forgive you and get on with the story.*

God *did* know what he was doing. You see, Satan told God that the only reason people served him was to get nice things from him. If God ever stopped blessing people, they would stop honoring him, Satan said. I can imagine the smirk on God's face as he was thinking, *Everybody's not like you, Satan. There are people who love and serve me even in the midst of trials and tribulations. I just pointed out one of them.*

So Satan took God up on his offer and Job's circumstances drastically changed. He went through a heart-wrenching, devastating hurricane of a process. He lost his servants, children, and livestock—all his earthly possessions except his wife. In the midst of this barrage, Job held fast to his trust in God and proclaimed, "Naked I came from my mother's womb, and naked I will depart. The LORD gave and the LORD has taken away; may the name of the LORD be praised" (Job 1:21).

Satan was perplexed. He and God had another conversation in which Satan argued that Job had not suffered enough. God allowed Satan to take another swing at Job by messing with his health. God told Satan he could touch Job's body, but not his soul. Satan was all happy about this because he believed that Job's health problems would surely make him turn away from God.

Job got boils and sores all over his body and started stinking and itching and scraping the scabs. His wife had all she could take and told Job just to curse God and die. Job had nobody left to help and care for him. And it didn't help matters when his friends came to visit. Bless their hearts, they thought they would sit with him for a week then open up a discussion to find out what Job had done wrong to deserve this kind of predicament.

Job was at the lowest point in his life. He said stuff like, "Why did I not perish at birth, and die as I came from the womb? . . . What I feared has come upon me; what I dreaded has happened to me. I have no peace, no quietness; I have no rest, but only turmoil" (Job 3:11, 25–26).

Poor Job not only was in a storm, he was in a sinking ship. And his friends were helping it go down.

Eliphaz, Bildad, and Zophar began a series of individual conversations in which they questioned Job's character and speculated that he must have done something awful to cause these things to happen to him. These "friends" accused Job of everything in the book in their attempts to explain his dilemma.

Job was beat down and asked for pity and for help from them. He knew he had not caused his plight. But he got no help from his friends. Instead, he gained strength from within when he said, "I know that my Redeemer lives, and that in the end he will stand upon the earth. And after my skin has been destroyed, yet in my flesh I will see God" (Job 19:25–26). Job asked God to curse him if he was guilty of any wrongdoing that had caused his situation. If God did not punish him, he knew he would be acquitted before his friends.

After another self-righteous friend, Elihu, accused Job of sin, Job really got down in the dumps. But God reminded Job of who the Almighty was and how he had performed wonders on the earth and in the sky, and even in Job's life. Job was sturdy enough to listen to God. He confessed his doubt and repented of his questioning. Then he made what I think of as his signature statement: "All the days of my hard service I will wait for my renewal to come" (Job 14:14).

Talk about hope in the midst of the storm!

God's mercy put that lowlife liar Satan back in his place. The waves calmed. The ship was balanced. The storm ended. God won!

People who really love God and trust him in the good times will also trust him in the bad times. Even though they may get weary and question why they are going through stuff, when the lightning bolts come out of the sky, they can always have hope that God will see them through their storms.

My most eye-opening discovery in reading this story is that Job died never knowing the deal God had made with Satan. He died never realizing why all this calamity had happened to him. All he knew was that he served a righteous God who cared for him, and he would forever trust the Lord, whatever happened in his life.

Many of us can relate to Job. We don't know why we have all these trials, and when our boat appears to be on the brink of shipwreck, we hear ourselves cry out, "I have no rest, but only turmoil!" But God does know what's going on, and he is working everything out for our good. When the storm rages and it seems like we'll be thrown overboard, our hope is in a Savior we can trust to save us from sinking.

～ *Dear Father, how comforting it is to know that when it appears we're about to sink in a sea of trouble, you are there to balance our vessel. Help us to keep in mind that Satan's attacks cannot destroy our hope and trust in you. Help us to look back at the storms you've brought us through and use those experiences as our barometer to measure your faithfulness to us. Amen.*

Safe in the Arms of Jesus

BARBARA JOHNSON

You will be secure, because there is hope;
you will look about you and take
your rest in safety. (Job 11:18)

*L*ast year as Operation Iraqi Freedom was getting started, a television reporter was interviewing military officers whose units had unusual assignments. The group that caught my attention had what you might call emergency respite duty. "We operate just behind the front lines," the officer explained, "and our job is to provide a place where soldiers can come out of the fighting for a while and rest. We set up tents and make them as dark and as comfortable as possible. We fill them with cots, and the soldiers come off the line to us as they can, day or night, to get some rest."

But it wasn't just the dark tents and waiting cots that created a safe haven for the soldiers coming off the front lines. It was their fellow soldiers' assurance that they were standing guard to protect them. "We tell the ones who come to us, 'You're safe here. You can rest now,'" the unit's commanding officer said. "'You get some sleep, and we'll keep you safe. That's why we're here—to make sure you're safe so you can sleep.'"

Certainly the guardians' words and provisions must have reassured the war-weary troops and helped create a safe haven for them. But I couldn't keep from speculating, as I listened to the report, that many of the exhausted soldiers probably took one more step as they settled down on their cots to rest. I suspected they whispered a prayer as they drifted off to sleep. Remembering what David wrote—"I will lie down and sleep in peace, for you alone, O LORD, make me dwell in safety" (Psalm 4:8)—I marveled at how we can find peace in the most unexpected places, knowing we are safe in the arms of Jesus. We know that no matter what happens to us here on earth, he has promised us an eternal home in heaven with him. That is the hope that helps us endure any trial.

After our son Steve was killed in Vietnam and his things were shipped home to us, we found a letter I had written him. It was in the jacket he had been wearing the day he died. The paper was stained with water from the rice paddy where he had fallen and was black with mold. But the lipstick kiss I'd put on it was still visible. Usually I wrote Steve letters full of jokes or funny tales about his brothers' latest pranks. But something—actually, I guess it was Someone—had moved me to write a different letter that day. It said:

> Steve, today I felt a special need to reaffirm our faith in eternal life and being prepared to meet God. I particularly wanted to assure you that whether you are at home here in West Covina or over there in Vietnam you are still SAFE in God's hands . . . and even if your life would be sacrificed for

us in Vietnam, EVEN THEN, Steve, you are safe in the arms of Jesus. . . .

Even death, should it come to us—ANY of us—brings us just a step closer to God and to eternity, because we have placed our faith in Jesus Christ.

What a comfort it was, after he was killed, to know Steve had carried that letter with him into battle, affirming to me that he clung to the same hope that has carried me through so many "battles" since then: the death of another son, Tim; the eleven-year estrangement of another son, David (whose relationship to us has now been restored); and, most recently, an ongoing war with a malignant brain tumor.

As Christians, we know we can face *anything* with courage and peace when we immerse ourselves in the hope of God's promises for our eternal future. Whether we're facing a military battle in the midst of war or a medical procedure in the midst of a health crisis or a raging storm within our families, we can know, without a doubt, that God will see us through it—and welcome us into his eternal "respite tent" when we leave the battle behind.

~ *Thank you, dear Lord, for the peace we have, even as storm clouds gather, because of your amazing, empowering, reassuring gift of hope. Amen.*

PART FOUR

Mayday!

Sending Up a
Distress Signal

SHEILA WALSH

~

*Then they cried out to the LORD in their trouble, and he
brought them out of their distress. He stilled the storm to a
whisper; the waves of the sea were hushed. (Psalm 107:28–29)*

When my son, Christian, began kindergarten in the
fall of 2002, life changed in our household. I am
not by nature a morning person, but I am now by necessity. I get
up at 6:00 every morning so that I can get myself together before
I wake him at 6:30. We are usually out the door by 7:20 so that
he can be seated in his classroom by five minutes to eight. We
have joined the military precision of the academic world.

During the first few weeks, I tried to gather as much information as I could from friends who are teachers. I wanted to be a
good "school mom." One of my friends, Sara, told me two things:
Make sure he has breakfast, and don't be late as it's embarrassing
for children to walk into the classroom when everyone else is
already seated. I etched those words on my heart.

One morning in the winter of 2003, I didn't wake up until
6:45. I yelped as I looked at the alarm and was in the shower

before I realized that I was out of bed. I woke Christian and told him that he had to have a shower today instead of a bath.

"But I want a bath, Mom," he said.

"We don't have time, sweet pea. Jump!" I looked at my wet hair and pulled on a ball cap. "Come on, Christian. We have to go!"

As we ran out the door, I grabbed the box of Cheerios and handed it to him.

"I don't want Cheerios today," he said. "I want toast soldiers."

"And I want to be five-foot-ten and Swedish, but it ain't going to happen," I replied.

"You're not supposed to say 'ain't,'" he whispered under his breath.

As soon as we turned out of our driveway onto the main street, I saw the traffic jam. Nothing was moving; the traffic was bumper to bumper. I tried to think of another route. There was a different way that we could take, but it was a lot longer. Not knowing why the traffic was stuck, I decided to try the alternate. As I attempted to stay at the speed limit, I watched the minutes ticking away. I became more and more anxious. We had ten minutes left to get to the school and we were at least twenty minutes away. When we pulled into the school parking lot, it was 8:15.

"Are we late, Mom?" Christian asked.

"We're a bit late, honey. I'm sorry," I told him.

"That's okay," he said as he pulled his backpack out of the backseat.

We had to report in at the front desk so that he could collect his "tardy" slip to give to his teacher.

"His class is already in chapel," the receptionist told me.

I had forgotten that this was Tuesday and chapel day for kindergarten through second grade. We dropped off his backpack in his classroom and made our way to the chapel door. Everyone was seated and listening to Mrs. Purdy, the elementary school headmistress. I looked to see where his teacher was and realized that Christian's class was sitting in the very front row. I watched my little lamb make his way to the front of the chapel, hand his slip to his teacher, and sit down. The back row of chapel was empty, so I plopped myself down too. Just then the music teacher began to lead the children in worship.

As their sweet voices filled the air, I sat and wept. I cried out to the Lord to help me. I was worn out by my internal struggle and anxiety. I was sad that Christian was late and it was my fault. I felt like a bad mom.

Looking back on it now, it seems silly to get so stressed out by a relatively small thing. But isn't it the small things in life that get to us? We are armed and ready for life's big blows and battles, but it's the little daily skirmishes, failures, or frustrations that can rob us of our inner calm.

As I sat in chapel on that winter morning, I sent up a distress signal: *Mayday, Lord!* Jesus stilled my inner storm to a whisper and hushed my surging soul as I listened to children lift their voices in praise to him.

~ *Father, thank you that when we cry to you, you hear our prayers and send your peace and grace to calm our inner storms. Have mercy on me today. Amen.*

Call God!

THELMA WELLS

~

Why are you downcast, O my soul? Why so
disturbed within me? Put your hope in God, for I will
yet praise him, my Savior and my God. (Psalm 42:5–6)

Some days this world seems to be just a big fat mess.
On the news we see footage of war and destruction.
People all over the country are being abused and misused,
many right in their own homes. Children are acting crazy.
Husbands and wives are abandoning each other and their kids.
Churches are in upheaval, just going through the motions of
worshiping God. Merciless killings and rampant crime plague
our communities. People are losing their jobs and the economy
looks like it's going rapidly down the tubes. It seems like more
people are physically sick today than ever before. In America,
the richest country in the world, there are folks going to bed
hungry and homeless. Schoolchildren have to pass through
metal detectors to go to their classroom, lunchroom, or library.
Drug and alcohol abuse is at an all-time high. Sexual perver-
sion, promiscuity, and pornography are destroying lives and
relationships.

I'll tell you, some days I wonder if we're in a submarine at the bottom of the sea, with no hope of seeing the sun on the water again.

What can we do when we feel like that? I've found a way to the surface. Repeat after me, and we can both be saved from our despairing moments: "God is our refuge and strength, an ever-present help in trouble" (Psalm 46:1).

When all I can see is trouble everywhere I turn, I review the names of God to remind me of his goodness and how worthy he is to be praised. Then I give him a call!

When you need God's power to help, call Elohim—God.

When you need the divine presence of God, call Yahweh—the Lord.

When you need the sacredness of God, call El Elyon—the Most High God.

When you need an overseer of your affairs, call El Roi—the God who sees.

When you need an all-powerful deity, call El Shaddai—God Almighty.

When you need a provider, call Yahweh Yireh—the Lord will provide.

When you need a helper, call Yahweh Nissi—the Lord is my banner.

When you need peace of mind, call Yahweh Shalom—the Lord of peace.

When you need a perfect Savior, call Qedosh Yisrael—God is morally perfect.

When you need a protector, call Yahweh Sabaoth—God is our Savior and protector.

When you need a God who will not die, call El Olam—the
everlasting God.

When you need a God of righteousness, call Yahweh
Tsidkenu—God is our standard for right behavior and
righteous living.

When you need a divine presence, call Yahweh Shammah—
the Lord is there.

When you need a God of ultimate authority, call Attiq
Yomin—the Ancient of Days, who will one day judge
the nations.

Right this minute I can feel refreshing air being pumped
into my spirit, lifting it from the bottom of the sea to the surface where the light of God is beaming down on the cabin of
my soul. My soul sings "Holy, Holy, Holy" to the Lord God
Almighty. The whole earth is full of your glory! Blessing and
honor, dominion and power be unto you, Most High God.
You are here for us in every area of our lives. Praise you
because you are worthy of our praise!

My soul is no longer cast down. I am no longer disturbed.
God has hoisted my soul from the depths to the light, by the
power of his name. My spirit is irrepressible because he has
filled it with hope. Hallelujah!

_Oh, Divine Master, it's so good to consider your name. Our only true
hope lies in your character. Any time we feel like we cannot rise above
the ocean floor, may your name fill our minds and lift our hearts in
praise. We appreciate the wonder-working power of your name, God
Most High. Amen._

The Not-So-Magnificent Obsession

NICOLE JOHNSON

I remember my affliction and my wandering,
the bitterness and the gall.
I well remember them,
and my soul is downcast within me.
Yet this I call to mind
and therefore I have hope:
Because of the LORD's great love we are not consumed,
for his compassions never fail.
They are new every morning;
great is your faithfulness.
(Lamentations 3:19–23)

To obsess— to think or worry about something
constantly or compulsively.

To think—to use the mind to consider ideas
and make judgments.

There is a big difference between thinking and obsessing.
Women can be very good at obsessing. Actually, anyone

can, but because we women carry so many things in our minds all the time, we tend to turn them over and over more frequently.

Thinking is like laying down a railroad track, using your mind to lay the groundwork for ideas and judgments to run on. Thinking is a constructive process. It's taking you somewhere, and you are making progress. Thinking has a sense of direction that guides you closer to where you would like to end up.

Obsessing, on the other hand, is like running on a hamster wheel. You are spending energy like you're really going somewhere, but in reality it's not possible. Obsessing is circular. It will take your energy and wear you out, but you will never end up any closer to a solution.

This contrast is described well in the above passage in Lamentations. The writer is confessing his obsessing. "I can't stop thinking about the past, about all the things I've done wrong, about how much I've messed up, how hard everything has been for me. I remember all that stuff and I can't get it out of my head. My soul is downcast within me and I can't think about anything else."

Sound familiar? For a lot of us, it does, because everyone has a past. Even a newborn has nine months of "past" when she comes into this world. The longer we live, the more we have behind us to make up that past. So it's easy to remember our wrongs more clearly than anything else because they have accumulated over the years. We can replay them like movies in our heads or flip through them in our minds like snapshots in a photo album. Or rehearse what we should have said like old lines in a script that we run over and over. But this is not thinking; it is obsessing. And it will never bring us closer to what we long for: closeness and connection to God. Mayday!

Look at what the psalmist says: "Yet this I call to mind, and therefore I have hope." What does he call to mind? Not the wrongs. Because obsessing over the past does not lead to hope. Just the opposite, in fact: It leads to despair. We begin the obsession cycle with thoughts like, *Nothing is ever going to change. Look what I've done. There is no way out. All is lost.* But real thinking counters all that with this powerful truth: God loves us. And because of God's love for us, we are not consumed.

When we are obsessing, we are in great danger of being consumed by our thoughts and feelings. We might let our fear overtake us or let our past get the best of us. But the writer tells us to stop obsessing and start thinking. Obsessing is not productive; it's destructive. It carves grooves in our minds that allow the tired scripts to keep running. Have you ever seen a dog that runs only on one little path in a yard and never veers off it? He creates a trail and digs it deeper and deeper by constantly running only on it. The whole yard is open to him to run and play, but he stays only on his little patch.

Thinking sets us free as we ponder God's love for us. It opens the whole universe to us instead of one little groove. It enables us to move forward in our lives toward the relationship with God that our hearts were made for.

God loves you . . . and that changes everything. Think on this and get off the hamster wheel. Start building the track of your life on God's love for you. His compassion doesn't run out. You can have real hope because God is faithful—even when you haven't been. He did not ask you to carry the burden of the faithfulness part; he promised to do that for you.

Get off the wheel and on the track!

~ *Lord, teach us how to remember our past without obsessing on it. Show us your love every day so our souls won't become downcast within us. Get us thinking about the right things so we can stop running old movies in our heads. Thank you that your compassions are new every morning. Great is your faithfulness. Amen.*

Lost and Found

BARBARA JOHNSON

Suppose a woman has ten silver coins and loses one.
Does she not light a lamp, sweep the house and search
carefully until she finds it? And when she finds it, she calls
her friends and neighbors together and says, "Rejoice with me;
I have found my lost coin." In the same way, I tell you, there
is rejoicing in the presence of the angels of God over
one sinner who repents. (Luke 15:8–10)

It was a dark day in the Johnson home. Bill and I were tearing the place apart—both in search of things we had lost. Of course *my* lost item was much more crucial than Bill's (at least in my opinion). It was my birthday book. Actually, it's an address book too; I just call it my birthday book because that was its original purpose. For years and years I've recorded all my friends' birthdays in it so I wouldn't forget them. And eventually, when I got smart, I started writing their addresses beside their birthdays so it would be easy to get a card ready to mail at the proper time.

The little book had become my precious companion, my source of vital information, my treasure trove of friends. All I had to do was open the book, and there were my friends, just a phone call or birthday card away. I had carried that book in my purse as I traveled around the country so that wherever I was speaking I could call up a friend and arrange a visit. But on that horrible "Mayday!" last year, my book had gone missing—and I had nearly gone out of my mind trying to find it.

Meanwhile, Bill had worked himself into a dither because he had lost a package of paper cups he'd bought at the warehouse store that morning. "I *know* I bought them—I've got the receipt right here," he fumed. "I *know* they were in the sack I carried out of the store. So where *are* they?"

Even though he eyed me suspiciously, he knew, deep down, that I was innocent. Still recovering from my latest round of chemo, I rarely ventured outside our home except to go to the doctor's office. So to Bill the awful truth was obvious: *He* had lost the cups.

I know I should have been more sympathetic. After all these years of being married to him, I know better than anyone that Bill is a dyed-in-the-wool perfectionist, an ex-navy man who has always insisted that everything be shipshape and properly stowed. I've seen firsthand how he suffers when something is misplaced—especially when he has to admit that *he* was the one who misplaced it! But on that long, frustrating day I was too consumed with my own frantic searching to think about his problem; after all, the birthday book was *much* more valuable than a silly package of cups!

We tripped over each other as we opened cabinet doors, pulled out drawers, and eased ourselves onto the floor to look under tables, couches, beds, and chairs. One after the other, we lifted the sofa pillows, peered behind the drapes, dug through the trash, and even checked the laundry hamper.

Our house isn't that big—we live in a mobile home. So after several hours of this futile searching in every nook and cranny, you might think we would have given up. But we didn't, although we paused a time or two to rest and gather our strength for the next attack. You see, we *knew* the lost items were there somewhere. So we never gave up hope of finding them. If I had been on a cross-country trip that week, I might have felt hopeless, fearing I'd left my precious birthday book on an airplane or in a hotel. But I hadn't been anywhere that week. So I kept on searching, knowing I *would* find what I'd lost.

Finally, I collapsed into my chair and heaved out a prayer of self-pity: "Oh, Lord, *you* know where my birthday book is. And I trust you to keep it safe until I can find it. I know you'll lead me to it. My hope is in you, Lord, in this little thing—and in *all* things."

For a few more minutes I sat quietly, letting my eyes scan the room. My focus kept coming back to the couch. I'd already looked under the couch and under its cushions. Still . . . as I thought back to where I'd last seen my birthday book . . .

"Bill, would you help me move the sofa?" I shouted out the door to the carport, where Bill was rechecking the backseat of the car, still on the trail of the missing cups.

"You already looked under it," he hollered back.

"Yes, but I want to look *behind* it," I answered.

He came in, a scowl on his face. He didn't like having his search-and-rescue mission interrupted. As he heaved the sofa away from the wall, I heard a soft thud. My precious birthday book had slipped off the back of the couch, where I'd left it, and come to rest behind the couch on the top of the baseboard, so I hadn't seen it when I'd looked underneath. As soon as the couch was moved away from the wall, it fell to the floor. I scooped it up and clutched it to my chest, hearing the strains of "Amazing Grace" waft gently through my mind. What once was lost had now been found.

Like the woman in Jesus' parable, I called all my friends and shared the happy news. And after I'd laughed over the silly incident with several of them, I settled down again for one more "call": "Thank you, Lord, not just for helping me find my birthday book, but for reminding me of your reassuring parable. Your Word fills me with hope in all circumstances, great and small, because no matter how the immediate situation turns out, I already know the final outcome. I know you will search for me if I lose my way. And on those dark days of my life when it feels like I've lost *you*, I'll never stop searching—because I *know* you'll be there. You have promised you will be."

P.S. Bill's still looking for those cups. He knows they're here somewhere . . .

⁓ *Dear Jesus, even if I lose everything else, I'll never lose hope— because* you *are my hope in all things. Amen.*

Kicking the Bucket Habit

MARILYN MEBERG

Two people can accomplish more than twice
as much as one. (Ecclesiastes 4:9 NLT)

"You're losing your mind," I muttered to myself.

"How could I be losing my mind?" I countered. "I'm only ten years old."

"Your Aunt Florence lost her mind when she was fourteen . . . maybe you're ahead of the game."

That thought put me in major "Mayday!" mode. I'd never worried about my mental health until Dad took two years away from his public ministry and bought forty acres of isolated property away from all living creatures except bears, cougars, deer, coyotes, and, on occasion, skunks. Appropriately, he named the remote retreat Lonely Acres.

It was on the advice of Dad's good friend Dr. Clark that we found our way to Lonely Acres. "You're killing yourself, Jasper," the doctor told my dad. "You'll have a heart attack and have an early death like your father did. Go back to the soil for a few years; it will heal your soul and strengthen your body."

With great exuberance Dad built a little house for us, started growing acres of hybrid blueberries, tended a pig whose mouth noises were appalling, and put a new roof on an old barn where several cows then took up residence.

While Dad healed, I declined. I tried to decline quietly; since Dad was doing so well, I didn't want to become a distracting source of concern. But before long it became obvious to my parents that their skinny daughter, who was eating less and less, was not making a good adjustment to life in the wild.

I became peculiarly obsessed with a fear of vomiting. (I had not vomited in years, though the fear was as great as if I did it every day.) To avoid vomiting, I did not want to eat anything but bread and milk, which I assumed would present minimal digestive challenge. Then I reached the point of not wanting to go to sleep without a bucket strategically placed by my bed in the event I vomited in the night. My parents were alarmed. One morning I heard them talking in hushed voices about Aunt Florence. Dad wanted to know at what age she exhibited the beginning signs of the schizophrenia that continues today to shroud her soul in anguish. Mayday!

Fortunately for me, school started and I was once again in the company of those who sported no discernable body fur and walked on two legs instead of four. Though I was greatly comforted to be with people again, I still needed the security of my well-placed bucket at night. My bucket need disappeared completely when Dad, fully restored, took the pastorate in a church in Vancouver, Washington. Leaving Lonely Acres and moving back into civilization was all I needed to kick the bucket habit. I haven't needed one since!

One of the most salient truths I've taken from my Lonely Acres days and my shiny bucket nights is, people need people.

Except for those rare few who are wired differently than most, or those who are temporarily peopled out as my father was, we benefit from the presence and support of other human beings. "Share each other's troubles and problems," says Galatians 6:2 (NLT). God made us to come alongside one another and enjoy our human relatedness.

I received a letter last week from a woman who has suffered from varying degrees of depression all her life. She has mustered the emotional energy to put together a little group of women who also are plagued by depression. They come together each week, share their souls, pray together, and drink coffee and eat cookies. She told me her new group has filled a need her medication was not able to touch. The group renewed her hope.

You may not have a bucket habit to kick, but you undoubtedly have other types of "Mayday!" experiences. Perhaps you've lost your hope. Invite God to meet you where you are. While you're talking to him, ask him to help you keep your eyes open for someone willing to "share your troubles and problems." Then . . . start baking cookies.

~ *Father, you offer hope in many different ways. Thank you that one of those ways is for us to come alongside each other and offer loving support. Amen.*

The Great Physician

THELMA WELLS

~

But for you who revere my name, the sun of
righteousness will rise with healing in its wings.
And you will go out and leap like calves
released from the stall. (Malachi 4:2)

The month of October used to be a joyous time for us in Texas because we anticipated attending the State Fair. My husband and I would take our children to the fair to ride the carousel and baby Ferris wheel. All was well until one October when our baby daughter became sick. We thought it was just a cold or allergies until we noticed her breathing hard. She was running a temperature. When we took her to the doctor, he had us rush her to the emergency room of the nearest hospital. Pneumonia had settled in our three-year-old's little lungs.

What? Now how did this happen? We took good care of our babies. We were with them all the time. This was devastating to us.

The medical people hooked our daughter up to an oxygen machine and other bottles, bags, and tubes. Trying to stick a needle in the arm of a toddler is as hard as trying to capture a hyper puppy. She flipped and flopped, squealing and squawking. Our hearts about broke.

I prayed for her, but not with the faith and fervency I would have had today. I was a Christian, but nothing like this had ever happened, and I hadn't heard a lot of talk about the healing power of God. Thank God she got well . . . for another year, that is.

The following October we were again preparing to go to the fair. We had not anticipated the identical thing happening just before Fair Day. We went through the same frightening ordeal.

What was happening? We did not see this coming on at all. The doctor told us that if we had not brought her to the emergency room when we did, she probably would have died. Died?! What was wrong?

Turns out she had asthma. We were not taught much about the disease. All we knew was to notice if she became short of breath. We did. We gave her prescribed medicine.

The next October we were more vigilant. Well, actually, we were afraid. We did not want to experience the same thing this year as we had the last two. We just wanted to take our little girl and little boy to the fair and have a good time. We bought the tickets and looked forward to the rides and fun.

Lo and behold, in the middle of the night before Fair Day, we heard wheezing and labored breathing. It happened for a third time: the emergency room, needles, tubes, bottles, bags, breathing apparatus, hospital stay.

My husband went to the fair by himself that year with one purpose: to win his little girl a big stuffed animal. He either won it or bought one, because he walked into the hospital room to present a beautiful white bear to his sick daughter. When the doctor saw it, he said she couldn't have it because it was furry and might cause her asthma to flare up.

During these hospital episodes I had seen my husband cry because his little girl was in agony. But this day I saw him cry and fume in frustration because there was absolutely nothing he could do to help her, not even give her a gift. The doctor told us that because she'd had pneumonia so many times, she would not be able to participate in strenuous activities when she started school. No running, dancing, sports, or physical activity of any kind. In gym she would need supervised rest because there was so much scar tissue on her lungs.

That must have been the gale that lifted me off my feet. I went from being somewhat passive about praying for my child's healing to storming the gates of heaven like a tornado. I had never prayed so hard for healing in my life. I had heard about God healing people, but I didn't know anyone who had been miraculously healed. I felt I had nothing to lose by asking God to heal my baby. I really had everything to gain. She was my heaviest burden, so I surrendered her to the Great Physician.

Several weeks after she was released from the hospital for the third time, the doctor called for me to bring her in for an appointment. When we finished the checkup, he sent us to the lab for x-rays of her lungs. We'd just returned home when he called for us to come back to the lab because the x-rays did not develop properly.

We hopped back in the car and headed for the lab. This

time, the doctor asked us to wait after the x-rays were taken until he had an opportunity to read the results. We waited the longest time. When he finally came out to give us the report, he said with astonishment, "There's no scar tissue. I could not find one bit of scar tissue. This is amazing. When we x-rayed her in the hospital, her lungs were so scarred I knew she would not be able to live a normal life. Now there's no scar tissue at all!"

A wellspring of joy and happiness sprung up in me and tears poured down my cheeks like a waterfall. Our child was well! God had answered my prayers! He had taken us across the miraculous bridge of hope and set us securely out of harm's way.

Since that day more than thirty years ago, I have never doubted God's miracle-working power. Though I know he heals in many different ways and doesn't always answer like I want, I believe to my bones that he hears when I call "Mayday!" He cares. He loves. And he *is* the Great Physician.

⌁ *Lord of love, we know that you have more healing in your garment than all the waters in the universe. Thank you for hearing and responding to our "Maydays!" Heal our bodies from sickness and disease. But most of all, heal our hearts of being timid and faithless where you are concerned. You are almighty! Praise your name. Amen.*

Drop Zones

LUCI SWINDOLL

~

Find rest, O my soul, in God alone; my hope comes
from him. He alone is my rock and my salvation; he is my
fortress, I will not be shaken. (Psalm 62:5–6)

On a flight to Oregon from California in July of 1989, I was seated in row 17 on the aisle, and breakfast had just been served. We had reached our cruising altitude of thirty-three thousand feet and were flying along nicely when all of a sudden two little girls across the aisle both screamed at the top of their lungs as the plane plummeted straight down. Breakfast trays went everywhere and yellow masks fell out of the ceiling as everybody looked aghast and confused. I began to pray as I reached up to take my mask and try to put it on.

The man next to me put on his mask and then said in a very calm voice, "There's nothing to be afraid of; we've hit an air pocket. Here, let me help you." I felt like the child in the flight attendant's speech when she says, "Be sure to put your mask on first, then . . ." This kind gentleman, whose breakfast tray had flown across my lap just moments before, said gently, "I'm a pilot, and the best thing to do is to be very still and breathe deeply. You'll be fine." As he spoke, he pulled the strap on my yellow face cup snugly. I can tell you I was *not* fine.

Momentarily, with coffee cups on the floor and food scattered about, flight attendants were holding on to whatever they could find. Just then, the captain came on and announced, "Ladies and gentlemen, we've just dropped twenty thousand feet in an air pocket. These things happen sometimes . . . nothing to be afraid of." *That's easy for him to say,* I thought. Everybody breathed a sigh of relief as he went on. "I call these pockets 'drop zones' because they come when least expected and you feel like you're going to fall out of the sky. But everything rights itself. We'll be back up to our cruising altitude in no time." There was something about his calm voice and reassuring words that helped me relax a bit.

We made it to our destination with no further mishap, and when we landed I looked back as I was deplaning. Dangling from the ceiling were all those strange little yellow masks. The sight was eerie and unforgettable. Since that day they have symbolized to me the "drop zones" in my life—times when I've been confused, hurt, brokenhearted, or downright scared. Times when my hope in the Lord was all I had to cling to.

I remember when my father had a stroke in church (while my brother Chuck was preaching). I was seated next to Daddy and motioned for Ken Meberg (Marilyn's husband, who was standing in the back) to come and help me with the situation. In no time he was there, had called the paramedics, and had everything under control. Chuck finished his sermon, as he knew Daddy would have insisted. Afterward, he met us at the hospital. The stroke led to a period of helpful hospitalization and a place to live after that with nursing assistance on a daily basis. Daddy's new home was only a few blocks from mine, so I could easily visit him regularly until the day he died, four years later. Those were some of our sweetest times together. God answered my prayers and gave rest to my soul as I hoped in him. For a few moments in the church pew, however, my heart hit a "drop zone" that was frightening and hard to climb out of.

Then there was the time two very dear neighbors moved from California to Florida. I was devastated. They weren't just neighbors but good friends, and my heart was broken as I wondered when we'd ever see one another again. I felt like they were moving to the other side of the world, not the other side of the country. I was so heartsick I cried for days. That was a very real "drop zone" for me, and my heart lived in my stomach for a while. After they left, however, we immediately planned visits and reunions, and we've been enjoying them ever since. Our friendship has grown much deeper over the past ten years of geographical separation. Our mutual commitment to each other and to the Lord has kept the relationship strong.

Drop zones can be mental, physical, emotional, or spiritual. And sometimes we feel them in all four areas simultaneously. They pull our spirits down and make us vulnerable to the enemy, who wants to steal our joy and peace. These are the times when hope in the Lord is invaluable. It protects our souls, lifts us up, and gives us a new way to look at the situation.

There's no way to keep the sky from falling and us going with it. No matter when this happens, we're never ready. But if we seek peace *in God alone,* he becomes a fortress in our darkest hour. He stabilizes us and gives us courage to keep going. He is our divine "Pilot" and seats himself right next to us at all times. Knowing he's there and will never leave us is the greatest hope of all.

~ *Lord Jesus, keep my eyes on you when I feel like I'm falling fast. My hope is in you alone. Amen.*

Hope Floats

NICOLE JOHNSON

*We are hard pressed on every side, but not crushed;
perplexed, but not in despair; persecuted, but not abandoned;
struck down, but not destroyed. We always carry around in our
body the death of Jesus, so that the life of Jesus may also be
revealed in our body. (2 Corinthians 4:8–10)*

These are such strong verses of hope, and yet the word *hope* is never mentioned. Look how the writer tells us the truth about their circumstances and then the condition of their hearts. This doesn't make sense in the mind of the reader. It actually creates more questions. The writer says, "We are hard pressed on every side, but not crushed," making us wonder, *Why not?* We are perplexed, but we are not in despair. *How come?* We are persecuted, but we do not believe we have been abandoned. *Oh, really?* We have even been struck down, but we are not destroyed. *How can you say that?*

Some days, we aren't sure we could say that. Our burdens seem too heavy. They weigh us down. Things happen in our lives and we feel crushed, abandoned, and even in despair—so why didn't these Christians? Because they had irrepressible hope. In the midst of the darkest circumstances, their hearts were lifted. Why?

Because hope floats. It has buoyancy to lift us out of our troubles. It gives us fresh air to breathe in the middle of the stench of pain. It bubbles up inside us, often when we least expect it, and bobs around in our hearts, giving us surprising joy.

In contrast, despair sinks. It's heavy. It has no air inside it. It's a weight like lead that presses down on top of our hearts. It feels like trying to swim with a bowling ball in your hand. You feel that at any moment you might drown under the weight of your circumstances.

Maybe the most beautiful thing about hope is that it is no respecter of circumstances. Real hope has very little to do with what is going on around us. But we continue to think it does. We believe, *If only our circumstances would change, we would really have hope.* It doesn't work that way.

Time and again I've seen people who have no reason to hope, floating on hope's uplifting support, keeping their heads way above water. I've seen this in an infirmary in Jamaica where the sick are left to die and in an AIDS house in India where women, not long for this world, are being cared for with their children. I will remember the people in these places for the rest of my life because of the powerful hope they cling to every day. They are lifted by the buoyancy of their belief, evidenced by their beautiful smiles and joyous spirits in the midst of devastating circumstances.

But I've also spent time with people who have every opportunity to let hope bring them to the surface who seem on the verge of drowning. These can be people who have means and influence, who are in good health, who can make all their own choices and set the course for their lives—and yet lack the strength of hope that would carry them through a day without depression or despair.

Neither hope nor despair ultimately comes from our circumstances. The body of water in which we are swimming makes no difference. It's no easier to float in fifty feet of water than in five, and a person can drown in just a few inches of water. Hope will lift or despair will drag down depending on what we hold in our hearts.

So we hold this hope: Christ died for us—therefore we can live. His death for our sin lifts our hearts out of the mire of guilt. His resurrection from death resurrects our spirits to eternal life. This truth is what floats. This is the hope that refuses to be submerged. It will not be held down for long by the oppression of despair. It will come bobbing to the surface, giving us something to hold on to above water, keeping us from going under. This is irrepressible hope.

～ *Lord, when we feel like we are drowning, point the way to hope. It floats, and it will hold us up. Your life and death and new life show us how to rise above our circumstances on the buoyant power of your truth. We need not be in despair. We need not feel abandoned. We have not been destroyed. Cut loose your truths that they might bob to the surface of our hearts . . . and we'll hold on. Amen.*

"This Ain't about Nothin'!"

THELMA WELLS

~

To the man who pleases him, God gives wisdom,
knowledge and happiness. (Ecclesiastes 2:26)

In our materialistic culture everybody I know is trying to accumulate stuff. Now I don't have a problem with stuff. If you don't believe me, come to my house and try to move around in the living room without stubbing your toe on the leg of a chair or bumping into the grandfather clock or stabbing yourself with the end of the dining table. I like clothes, cars, diamonds, furs, and all that stuff. Except now that I'm over sixty-one years old, those things don't mean as much to me as they used to. (Well, I hope one day to be the proud owner of a three-carat marquise diamond with baguettes floating around it. But if I don't get it, I'll be just fine.) I really hope to have wisdom enough to know when enough stuff is enough.

In Scripture we read about this king named Solomon who just didn't know when he had enough. The wisest man to ever live. The richest man to ever live. And the most foolish man to ever live. What a paradox.

When God asked what he most wanted in life, Solomon asked for wisdom. He even wrote, "The fear of the LORD is the beginning of wisdom" (Proverbs 9:10). After some years, however, the king seemingly forgot about his fear of the Lord and stupidly disobeyed God by intermarrying with pagan idol worshipers and adopting their style of worship. That was foolish!

Solomon's mind got warped. His vision for the things of God got dim. His obsession with wickedness increased. His love for life drowned. His attitude got as rank as seaweed. Solomon had been dragging his nets in the wrong body of water. The king tried everything to feel better, but no matter what he experienced, owned, or controlled, it all seemed worthless and meaningless, empty and unsatisfying. He said, "I have seen all the things that are done under the sun; all of them are meaningless, a chasing after the wind" (Ecclesiastes 1:14). Solomon was depressed!

Do you ever get depressed like that? I've had some of the same thoughts when life isn't going my way. But I soon get over myself, because I've learned, like Solomon did, that there is a God-ordained time in life for everything to happen. We live in seasons of joy and sorrow, plenty and need, health and sickness, peace and trouble, strength and weakness, hope and despair. The stabilizing truth is this: "To the man who pleases him, God gives wisdom, knowledge and happiness."

Next time you're sitting and looking out at your river of material things, position, associates, activities, and assignments, and you find yourself thinking, *This ain't about nothin'!*—take heart. You are not alone. God has already been through all that with the wisest guy who ever lived—and a bazillion other beloved fools like you and me. We have a heavenly Father who will shower down meaning like manna on the nothingness we feel. When all our "stuff" loses its buoyancy and the meaning of life seems to sink to the bottom of the sea, we need only send up a "Mayday!" to Almighty God. He will remind us what we're really here for: to please him and enjoy his company. When we look for our meaning in him instead of in "stuff," he will make life worth living again.

~ *Creator God, you made all the stuff, and everything you made is good. Help us to put things in the right perspective. Help us to understand that the things we acquire and the things we desire are not for our glory but yours. Help us to be thankful for every good and perfect gift. And, Lord, when we get so full of ourselves that we think we're on our own down here, pull us back from the deck rail and sit us down for a good talking-to. Remind us that the beginning of wisdom is honoring you. Amen.*

Knock, Knock

PATSY CLAIRMONT

~

For behold, the winter is past, the rain is over and gone. The flowers have already appeared in the land. (Song of Solomon 2:11–12 NASB)

When I opened my front door in Michigan, I was surprised to find two young neighborhood girls with sweet smiles holding a festive basket. "Mrs. Clairmont, we wanted to wish you and Mr. Clairmont a happy May Day and give you these flowers."

I was delighted. In all my years I had never had anyone present me with a May Day basket. What a cheery way to start a day and celebrate a month. May Days in Michigan are full of hope because finally we see signs of spring's progress over our tenacious winters. Like confetti over a parade, the infusion of color and beauty makes it impossible not to join in the celebration. Crocuses, daffodils, and tulips hold their own as they seem to shout triumphantly across our once gray landscape, "We win! We win!"

But I've had other Maydays. Times filled with tension and dissension where even in the midst of a garden the heart can wilt . . .

One particular day, instead of finding flowers when I answered my door, I found an angry friend with a basketful of hostility. One who had been offended by me and had come by to tell me so. The relationship was important to me and I very much wanted to resolve the conflict, but the longer she talked the bleaker the landscape of our friendship appeared. It felt as though every stony word she spoke added heaviness to my heart. By the time she left, I was drowning in a sea of confusion, weighed down by her accusations and innuendos, and defeated by what felt like the hopelessness of it all. After several sleepless nights and fretful days, I could tell that I was emotionally in over my head. Finally, I put out a "Mayday! Mayday! Mayday!"

My friend Pat, who happens to be a therapist, greeted me warmly when, like a waif, I showed up at her front door. I was a basket case. Pat allowed me to rattle on for a while, and then she began to help me sort out the conversation and my feelings. Truth was, my angry friend was right about a number of things, and I had to own up to that. But she was wrong about some other things, and I had to emotionally shake those off and let them be hers. By the time I left Pat's, my soul was lifted. Her wise counsel helped me hurdle the growing despair I was feeling, and her willingness to let me rattle out my tale was liberating. Sorting out the muddle in my mind by verbalizing to Pat what had happened was like stepping from the gloom of winter into the light of spring.

What is there about hope that leaves us so, well, hopeful? I guess knowing there's a way out, a way through, and a way at all. Perhaps that is why Jesus reassured us with, "I am the way and the truth and the life" (John 14:6). He knew we would need to have our hopes pinned on him if we were to remain hopeful, because people and situations are constantly in flux. Even the best of relationships will suffer conflict, even the surest financial arrangements can go bankrupt, and even the safest circumstances can turn risky. But Jesus remains eternally the same: a sure way.

My grandson Justin is two and a half and loves the slide—that is, until he gets to the top of the steps. There he lets out a screeching "Mayday!" that can be heard throughout three states. Justin not only won't go down the slide, but he also won't come back down the steps without assistance. So there little Mr. Mayday remains, awaiting a rescuer's hand to help him down.

I understand the paralyzing realization that as much as I want to there are just some things I can't do alone. I wrote these lines for Justin . . . and me . . . and maybe you.

Be not afraid my little one,
Your head up in the sky.
The journey is a steady one—
On that you can rely.

Trust the one who holds your hand;
Take a risk, take a stand.
Scoot ahead—you're almost there;
Live your life with holy flair.

Look to those who've gone before,
Who've paved the way
To help you soar.
You're on the edge; there's so much more.

Be not afraid my little one,
Your head up in the sky.
The journey is a ready one,
And you're about to fly!

If hope could fit in a basket, I'd deliver one to your door today!

~ *Thank you, Jesus, for continually knock, knock, knocking at our doors. May we be astute enough to fling open the doors and receive all the bouquets of hope you offer. And thank you for responding to our "Maydays!" Because of you we can joyfully shout, "We win! We win!" Amen.*

PART FIVE

All Hands on Deck

People Need People

PATSY CLAIRMONT

～

Put on a heart of compassion. (Colossians 3:12 NASB)

People need people. It's our design. As we step through our assigned days on this terra firma or are tossed about on the high seas, we find ourselves crisscrossing the paths of many. At times we will invest in them and they in us. There will be days when folks will get on our last nerve and we will in return drive them banana crackers. We will touch some lives for only moments while others we will walk with as long as there is breath in our bodies. We will work alongside comrades, play next to others, worship with many, dine with some, and live with a few folks before we depart to shores even more populated. Even if we wanted to be a hermit (and sometimes that thought skitters across our minds), it would be tricky because the earth is jam-packed with folks and their cotton-pickin' relatives. (Smile.) Why, even our waterways require lanes and traffic laws to prevent boat jams and accidents.

For a while the other day I watched the Americas sailboat race on television, and quite honestly I didn't get it. One thing was for sure: The crew was busy. All hands were on deck hoisting and lowering sails, or cranking, uh, cranks first in one direction and then the other, while some stood aft calculating.

Now I can be cranky without much of an effort, and I'm good at standing, but don't ask me to calculate. I don't do numbers beyond my age and even that is starting to add up to figures higher than I'd like to be involved with. One thing I clearly observed about the Americas race was that you had to be skilled in your area and willing to be wholeheartedly involved. It was an all-or-nothing commitment.

Hmm, that's true of the Christian journey as well. Listen afresh to what Jesus asks of us: "'You shall love the Lord your God with all your heart, and with all your soul, and with all your mind, and with all your strength.' . . . 'You shall love your neighbor as yourself'" (Mark 12:30–31 NASB). Well, I'm exhausted. "All" is everything, right? How could such a little word be packed so full? And then the Lord throws in our need to love our neighbors. Now that, girlfriend, is a full-time assignment in itself.

Actually, I've been told that I'm a full-time assignment. I know it's true. I tend to be labor-intensive. At first it was little things like I needed help with locating my car keys. Then it grew, as I could never find my eyeglasses. Next it was my elusive purse, and more recently someone is vaporizing my car in parking lots. I seem to need more than a few people; as dingy as I am, I need an entire crew just to round up my paraphernalia. *Sigh.*

But that's truly the small stuff of life. And while we appreciate folks who are kind enough to help us get our act together, the ones who take our breath away are those who wholeheartedly show us the love of Christ when they risk coming aboard our boat in the midst of thrashing whitecaps and violent lightning strikes that threaten our very existence.

I have a darling new friend in my life, Sheila Soetaert. Sheila has been teaching me how to sail when caught in a wailing storm. She is a true-grit sailor. The gale-force winds of cancer have been threatening to capsize her vessel for some time. Sheila has learned to turn her sails until she catches the wind and allows it to be part of her momentum. She has been valiant, and many have come to help her batten down the hatches: her darling husband, her seven-year-old daughter, Chloe, other family members, her church, her support group, medical personnel, and so on. Sheila is grateful.

Recently Sheila was told that the raging seas will soon grow still and she'll be able to rest in the safety of the Lord's harbor. And as is the way of Sheila's Captain, he sent her yet another sailor to assist in this transition.

Sheila first met Annie at the hospital where Annie worked as an oncology nurse. The next time Annie and Sheila's paths crossed was at the church Sheila attended and where Annie had come to visit. Upon seeing each other again, they enjoyed, as they visited, a fast-growing friendship. Soon the two grew to be sisters of the heart. One day Annie told Sheila that when it was time for Sheila to make her way toward shore, she (Annie) would leave her job at the hospital and physically care for her.

In recent days Annie has done just that. Annie resigned her position and has climbed into Sheila's boat.

People need people.

~ *Lord, thank you for all the compassionate Annies who demonstrate the love of Christ on our storm-tossed seas. And thank you for sailors like Sheila who wholeheartedly sail on while heading toward a certain shore. Amen.*

My Big Fat Porch Family

LUCI SWINDOLL

~

*Be joyful in hope, patient in affliction, faithful in
prayer. Share with God's people who are in need.
Practice hospitality. (Romans 12:12–13)*

O ur first Women of Faith Conference in 2003 took us
to Sacramento, California, a place we all love. It's the
capital of my state, a beautiful city, and a wonderfully enthu-
siastic audience. I even have a dear friend who lives there. That
was the year of "The Great Adventure" theme. Little did I
know my own adventure would take an interesting turn that
weekend.

The conference went well; the nearly twenty thousand
women at the Arco Arena responded marvelously to our
brand-new conference, and we were ecstatic. I, however, felt
exceedingly tired by noon Saturday—much more than ever
before. And by that night, when I finished speaking and sign-
ing books, I was literally exhausted. *What's wrong?* I kept wondering. I heard myself say over and over, "I'm *so tired.*" I'm
sure people were thinking, *Hello! We're* all *tired.*

After the event on Saturday, the Women of Faith team is
always eager for a lively visit, a leisurely dinner in our hotel,

and a time to debrief. In light of the way I was feeling, however, it would have been the better part of wisdom for me to excuse myself from dinner and go straight to bed. But no! I certainly wasn't going to be a party pooper after the first conference, knowing we had twenty-eight to go!

No sooner had I gotten seated at the table than I began to perspire. When I asked the friend next to me if she thought I had a fever, she said, "No, but you're so clammy. Let me take your pulse." She couldn't find it. This frightened her—and others at the table. I lost all sense of what was going on around me. I didn't faint but might as well have. Before I knew it, I was lying on the floor with a nurse from a nearby table kneeling over me. Someone in the group was praying aloud. It was like watching a movie—only in this case I was the star, not the spectator.

Ultimately, the paramedics came, put me on a gurney, and whisked me away to nearby Sutter General Hospital. In the ER, the doctors determined that I was experiencing something called atrial fibrillation. This condition, in which the heart beats irregularly, can cause chest pain, shortness of breath, lightheadedness, and extreme fatigue—all of which I was feeling. While this wasn't a heart attack or stroke or even an uncommon problem, it was new to me and very scary to my friends.

So here I was, hardly knowing what was going on around me, with IVs in both arms, oxygen in my nose, my dear friend Mary Graham by my side, and the prospect of spending a night or even more in a strange hospital. I had no idea at that moment what had actually happened, nor if my condition was serious. Nonetheless, I had complete peace. It was the oddest thing, but I found the experience more interesting than frightening. I asked a thousand questions of the doctors, nurses, technicians, nurses' aids, custodians . . . any poor soul who crossed my path.

I now realize I was never in any real danger, and the extensive battery of tests that followed that little episode confirmed the positive news about what good health I enjoy. In the midst of that ordeal, however, I learned something I hope never to forget. I learned that God is near in times of trouble. Of course I know that. I preach it! But lying on that floor, in that ambulance, and in those unfamiliar surroundings at a Sacramento hospital, I learned God *really is* there.

Mary looked at me very tenderly at one point and asked, "Are you scared?" Without even thinking about what I was saying, I heard my voice respond, "No . . . the Lord is my strength." Quite honestly, I didn't feel a trace of fear. Not once.

The other memorable, and fantastic, part of the whole episode was the amazing, endearing, unparalleled love of my friends. Talk about attentiveness. Mary never left my side. For three days and nights she stayed with me in the hospital. When I was first taken behind the emergency room doors, she found a way to get past those bolted doors and never left.

While I was in the ER, a nurse asked me, "So . . . you have a big family, huh?"

"Big family? No, not too big . . . why do you ask?"

"Well, they're all in the waiting room trying like everything to get back here."

"Oh . . . *that* family. That's my big fat porch family. Yeah . . . it's really big."

On Sunday my "porch family"—Patsy, Marilyn, Sheila, Thelma, and Nicole—prayed for me, called to see how I was doing, and kept vigil over Mary and me hour by hour. By the time I finished my tests and procedures that afternoon, the whole "family" and other dear friends had shown up. The nurses were cautioning me to stay quiet, but my heart monitor revealed that I was higher than a kite. So much for prescribed rest!

We laughed and talked, told stories, joked, sang and praised God, and all but danced. (Had I been free of those IVs, I would have!) My pals' visit and their unspeakable care lifted my spirits like nobody's business. Hope *filled* the room. It was irrepressible—and so was I. A couple of people had cameras and took a bunch of pictures to record the adventure.

All this happened long before I had any definite information on my condition or how my health might be affected in the days ahead. I knew nothing except that God sent me these wonderful, warm, wacky, wild, sweet women—my porch pals. They stayed as long as they could, until finally and reluctantly, I had to let them go. Only after they all saw me with their own eyes in such good hands and great spirits were they willing to leave Sacramento.

When I finally went home two days later, with Mary and Marilyn by my side, I not only felt better, but my heart was literally palpitating with gratitude for who God is to me, how closely he abides, and what great gifts I have in those who love me. While I was "patient in affliction," as Paul writes in Romans 12, my friends were "practicing hospitality." While I was "joyful in hope," they were "faithful in prayer." They shared their love, kindness, grace, and time with me in a way I will never forget.

This is for them. It's my letter of thanks for all the hopefulness they brought to this old fibrillating heart when I was "afflicted" and for the love and joy they give me year after year after year.

My big fat porch family! Thank you. You're the *best*.

~ *Bless all those in this family of friends, Lord—and those in every family who know how to love and care for others. May we all practice the hospitality and faithfulness that you model for us. Amen.*

Radiating Hope

BARBARA JOHNSON

*Let him bury his face in the dust—there
may yet be hope. (Lamentations 3:29)*

When a loved one is facing a difficult challenge, sometimes the smallest, most insignificant things we do can give them hope—or push them into despair. That's why it's so important to consider carefully—and pray mightily about—the ways we reach out to those in need.

For example, Lisa, a single mother from Texas, described how hard—but how important—it was for her to maintain her physical appearance when her teenage daughter was diagnosed with a malignant tumor on her kidney.

"I'll admit it. I've been rather vain all my life," Lisa explained. "It has always been important to me to have my nails done and my hair styled. I'm one of those silly women who wouldn't think of stepping outside, even to pick up the newspaper, without putting my makeup on first. It's ridiculous, I know. But it's just the way I am. For as long as I can remember—even after the kids came along—my daily routine has been to head right for the shower the minute I get up in the morning. I put on my makeup, blow-dry my hair, and *then* head for the kitchen to start the coffee."

That practice changed the day her daughter's tumor was diagnosed.

"One minute we were in the doctor's office, and the next thing I knew I was in the hospital, kissing Brittany good-bye as she was wheeled away into surgery," she said. The operation took several hours and lasted until after midnight. The weary mother spent the night pacing the floor of the waiting room outside the intensive care unit. It was nearly noon the next day before she was able to see her daughter again.

When Brittany awoke and saw her anxious mother standing there, her clothes disheveled and her hair unkempt, her mascara smeared and her cheeks colorless, Brittany's eyes filled with fear. "Mama, am I going to *die?*" the girl asked.

Although her daughter's prognosis wasn't at all certain, Lisa hurried to reassure Brittany. "Oh, no, honey! You're gonna get better. I'm sure of it."

Later a nurse came out to the ICU waiting room and gently took Lisa aside. "Brittany seems sure she's going to die," the nurse told her. "And as strange as it seems, apparently it's because you aren't wearing lipstick."

"What are you talking about?" Lisa asked incredulously.

"Well, it isn't just lipstick. I hope you won't mind my saying this," the nurse continued, a little hesitantly, "but Brittany told us, 'I know I'm dying, because my mother would *never* be seen in public looking like that unless something really, *really* awful was happening.'"

Lisa, who at that moment had lost all interest in wearing makeup and didn't care if her hair was ever combed again, dropped her head in misery.

"Go home," the nurse said. "Take a shower. Get a little rest. Pull yourself together. Everything is going to be okay."

Lisa did as the nurse suggested, and when she returned to the hospital that afternoon, she wore her brightest outfit and her most carefully applied makeup and made sure every hair was in place. Brittany's face brightened when she saw her mother. "Oh, Mama," she said, smiling, "you're beautiful again."

After that, even though she sometimes felt guilty about the time it took for her "beauty routine," Lisa never showed up at her daughter's bedside without looking her best. By presenting a consistent image to Brittany, she helped reassure the girl that her case wasn't hopeless. Simply by continuing to do what she had always done, she gave her daughter hope.

Now this emphasis on appearance may seem silly to you, especially if you've never worn makeup and you don't own a blow-dryer. But the point is, this mother learned what gave her daughter hope, and she did what was needed to keep that message alive. The lesson reminds me of how airline passengers instinctively look around for the flight attendants when turbulence suddenly sends the airplane dipping and bucking through stormy skies. If we see that the flight attendants, despite the roller-coaster ride, are sitting in their jump seats chatting away as usual, chuckling about a shared joke or nodding knowingly as a point is made, we feel confident that everything's okay, despite the bumps. On the other hand, if we see them sitting silently, focused on each bump and swoop, with all the color drained from their faces and their lips pressed tightly together into a thin, firm line, we start to think the end is near.

It would be great if we could always be prepared to share hope through eloquent speaking and biblical mentoring; how nice if we could have Scripture verses memorized and beautiful prayers prepared to share at a moment's notice in the most frightening situations. But the truth is, sometimes we share hope without saying a word. Sometimes we inspire others to hold on in frightening circumstances simply by continuing to live as though the circumstances *aren't* frightening—as though we know everything's going to be all right.

Because we do! That's the hope God has given us. He has promised to use everything that happens in our lives for our good. And he has promised that on the other side of the earthly trials that confront us, heaven awaits. So we know, as someone said, everything will be okay in the end. If it's not okay, it's not the end!

God's promises give us the confidence and reassurance we need to bring hope to others, whether it's in the words we say, in the actions we take, or in the peaceful beauty of his empowering love we wear on our faces.

⌒ *Dear Father, let your love fill our lives so thoroughly that we radiate hope wherever we go, whatever we do—even in the most hopeless circumstances. Amen.*

Love One Another

SHEILA WALSH

A new command I give you: Love one another. As I have loved you, so you must love one another. By this all men will know that you are my disciples, if you love one another. (John 13:34–35)

I looked out of the airplane window as we began to circle Glasgow, Scotland. I hadn't been home for four years, and now as I looked out at the green grass and the hills, I felt the quiet peace that home means to me. Christian was two on our last trip, so he had no memories of his visit. Now, at six, he was revved up and ready to go.

"Who'll meet us, Mom?" he asked.

"Aunt Frances, Uncle Ian, and perhaps David and John," I told him.

"What are my cousins like?" he wanted to know.

"Well, David is twenty-one," I said. "He's at Stirling University and he plays guitar. John is eighteen and he's not quite sure yet what he wants to do. He might go to Bible college."

The plane landed and we made our way to baggage claim. I saw my sister first. I love Frances. She is two years older than I, sweet and funny and very opinionated (it must run in the family). Then I saw Ian, her husband. Barry and I love him as if he were our own brother. We hugged and then I saw a strange look on Christian's face. He had just caught sight of David and John. I must say that I found the experience breathtaking too. David is now six-foot-five-inches tall with long hair. John is about six feet tall and had dyed his hair bright red.

"Are those my cousins?" Christian whispered.

"They are," I replied, wondering how he would receive the news.

"Cool!" he cried out as he ran to hug them.

He became like a little puppy at their feet for the rest of the trip. He was so relieved that there are some "cool" people in our family. They were so sweet to him. David let Christian play his precious electric guitar and gave him a private concert, and John endured hours of being pounced on, asked questions, hugged, and generally harassed.

It was one of the sweetest Christmases I can remember. On Christmas Day we gathered with Frances's family, our mom, and Ian's parents.

"This is going to be easy," Christian whispered in my ear before we sang the blessing.

"What will, darling?" I asked him.

"Loving my family."

May that always remain a reality in his life!

But it's not always easy, is it? We disappoint each other so routinely, and sometimes a family holiday like Christmas can be one of the hardest times of the year as we open one more round of strange gifts that seem to say to us, "See, they don't know you at all!" But the pattern Christ set for us on his voyage in human flesh was to love freely without demanding anything in return. He poured out his life and his love wherever he encountered brokenness and need. And he told us that we must love one another as he loved us.

Those are strong and demanding words, for how can we love as Christ loved? The reality is that we can't in our own strength; such love is simply not in us. But Christ doesn't ask that we muster up this stuff by ourselves; rather, he simply asks that we allow him to love through us.

There are many stories told of friends and family members who come to Christ, drawn by the change in someone they thought they knew so well and yet who has been transformed by the love of God. Some of Kate B. Wilkinson's hymn lyrics inspire me to follow Jesus' "new command."

> May the love of Jesus fill me
> As the waters fill the sea;
> Him exalting, self abasing—
> This is victory.
>
> May I run the race before me,
> Strong and brave to face the foe,
> Looking only unto Jesus
> As I onward go.
>
> May His beauty rest upon me
> As I seek the lost to win,
> And may they forget the channel,
> seeing only Him.

Father, teach me to love as you love. Give me your eyes to see and your ears to hear. May the mind of Christ dwell richly in me. Amen.

The Magic of Music

LUCI SWINDOLL

❦

He put a new song in my mouth, a hymn of praise
to our God. Many will see and fear and put
their trust in the LORD. (Psalm 40:3)

We were just shy of our teenage years when my brothers and I dared to take out a little skiff on the bay one afternoon when we were visiting at my grandfather's cabin. It was summer vacation. We fished and swam and picnicked and loved it all. But it wasn't enough. We wanted to throw in a little dangerous living. So we rowed an ill-equipped, scruffy, poorly built boat about a hundred yards out from shore and were having the time of our lives cavorting around, when suddenly we realized there were several holes in the bottom of the boat and it was filling with water.

Mayday! With what we had—a rusty tin can, our tennis shoes, and our hands—we frantically began to bail water as fast as we could. Chuck decided to jump out and try to pull the boat to shore as Orville and I dumped as much water as we could overboard.

Somehow, in the jump Chuck caught the back of his leg on a nail protruding from the boat and ripped a gash in it the size of Arkansas. He yelled that something was wrong, but I just kept telling him to pull. *Pull. Pull.* When we finally made it to shore, I could see that Chuck had indeed hurt himself badly. We all ran to the house to show Mother the damage to her youngest child. I felt guilty we'd committed such a criminal act, that Chuck had been truly injured, and that I had ignored his yelling. He'd lose his leg for sure because I'd been such a creep.

Without a shred of panic, Mother immediately washed the injury with soap and water, applied medicine, and then bandaged it up. When Chuck got his bearings and Mother finished her nursing task, she quietly began to sing. Of all things! It was a hymn. Soon we'd all joined in, and the tension surrounding the trauma began to fade. For the first time I felt like Chuck would live, maybe even get better, and everything would improve as long as the family took care of each other and we sang together. (And this was *before* the days of *Little House on the Prairie*.) The music buoyed our spirits. There was a feeling of "overcoming" in the room that started with Mother singing that hymn.

I can't remember a day in my childhood when the strains of music were not heard throughout our house. Either Orville was playing the piano in the living room or Mother was singing in the kitchen. Chuck was tooting out a melody on his clarinet or Daddy was treating us to one on his harmonica. I even chimed in from time to time with my ukulele. This was a ragamuffin, get-down, hang-loose, give-it-your-all *family band*. We didn't care if the neighbors heard us or not. We weren't trying to be good. We were just having fun. Music was in our souls, and it had to come out.

And sing? Oh, my! Church choirs, glee clubs, quartets, trios, solos . . . you name the group, we were in it. Since Daddy couldn't carry a tune in a bucket, he stuck to his harmonica or turned the pages when we had to follow a score.

There was something about these musical family gatherings that helped us cope with everyday life and sent us on our way knowing hope was in the air and all was right with the world. Even if it wasn't. I learned it as a child, and I practice it as an adult. To this day, if I'm riding in a car with one of my brothers and start singing, whichever one of them is with me will join in, in harmony.

I can recall many situations in which music took tension, boredom, anxiety, or sadness out of the air. It not only took it away, it substituted it with a spirit of hopefulness.

In the early 1960s when I was singing with the Dallas Opera Chorus, I had been selected to be in a small group onstage as the family of *Madame Butterfly*. Naturally, I was thrilled and excited about this opportunity. We got together to practice each Friday night after work in the hotel room of the opera prompter, as the rest of the singers worked in another building with the chorus master.

On this particular Friday, everybody was dead tired after a week's work at our various jobs, and the singing was downright awful. Having to perform in Italian and assimilate what the words meant was bad enough, but we had to be *on pitch*. This was too much to ask. Everybody was weary, out of sorts, mad at each other and the conductor—too discouraged to go on. We couldn't even sit up straight.

With no announcement or fanfare, our conductor suddenly

got up from his chair, turned off the lights in the room, opened the drapes so we could see the twinkling lights of the city, and went to the piano. He began playing an Italian love song. It was beautiful. And soon, he began to sing (in Italian, of course). Every one of us sat stone silent as we were transported to another place for maybe fifteen minutes. I had no idea what the man was singing, but in my mind's eye I could picture a gondola gliding through the waters of a Venice canal, or a balcony in Florence where lovers were talking and kissing, or a family in Rome sitting around a table of homemade pasta and laughing a lot. It was absolutely mesmerizing and wonderful. The conductor didn't have a very good voice, nor did he play piano all that well. But he knew the magic of music.

When he stopped, we all jumped to our feet and began applauding—rejuvenated. After a bit of visiting and verbal appreciation for that incredible respite, the rehearsal began again and we all sang beautifully—and on pitch! We even laughed and teased and followed every measure of the score as though we'd been singing it for years.

Music gives us irrepressible hope. It fills cathedrals with praise and thanksgiving to God for his provision, protection, and peace. It leads a marching band in the anticipation of victory. It enables a mother to comfort her baby as she rocks him to sleep. It permits a jazz pianist to get everybody in the joint toe tappin' and finger drummin' to the rhythm of the beat. We feel the hope and joy in our joints and limbs as the music comes through our pores. We're good. Bold. Free. "We'r gonna make it" takes over and the blues melt away.

The next time you discover holes in the bottom of your

boat and you feel like you're going to sink, don't despair. God will bail you out. You just keep singing.

〜 *Heavenly Father, put a song in my mouth today—one that will remind me that you're the Captain and I'm just the sailor. You're the trustworthy one, and I'm the one who's trusting. Give me your hope and peace, Lord, in Jesus' name. Amen.*

Who You Gonna Call?

BARBARA JOHNSON

*Answer me, O LORD, out of the goodness of
your love; in your great mercy turn to me. Do not hide
your face from your servant; answer me quickly, for
I am in trouble. (Psalm 69:16–17)*

It used to strike me as funny every time I would see the
little box on the front page of the newspaper that said, "If
your newspaper isn't delivered, call this number." *If your newspaper hadn't been delivered, you wouldn't have the number to
call,* I mused. Then someone pointed out that you could look
at yesterday's newspaper to find the number.

Yesterday's newspaper? I thought. *You mean in some house-
holds yesterday's newspaper is allowed to hang around for another
twenty-four hours?*

At our house, Bill is so compulsive about keeping everything neat and tidy that I sometimes have to carry the paper
around with me during the morning as I move about the
house just to make sure he doesn't snatch it away and tie it up
in the recycling bin before I get a chance to read it.

Nearly every product these days has a phone number
printed on the label, so you can make a quick call if something

goes wrong with a loaf of bread you've bought or you aren't sure how to use a bar of soap or a ballpoint pen. It's reassuring to know help is just a phone call away. But there's one little catch. You have to have that specific number—the help-line number. (For me, that's a *big* catch, because if you think Bill is quick to get rid of today's newspaper, you should see how fast things like soap wrappers and pen packaging disappear at our house!)

Last year I lost my credit card, and I didn't know whom to call. First, I tried the number I found in the phone book. After listening to a mind-numbing menu of possibilities, none of which mentioned credit cards, I finally got to speak to a human being—who told me to call another number. That launched the whole menu-option recital again, and once again there was nothing about reporting lost credit cards. By the time I'd heard the whole list, I'd forgotten which number to push for the option that had sounded like it might have a remote potential for helping me.

Finally, I called the bank that had issued the card. Six menu options later, I was once again speaking to a real person. But if that lady had come with her own personal list of menu options, "helpfulness" would not have been one of them.

"Just call the number on the back of the card," she told me hurriedly.

"Excuse me?" I asked.

"If you'll turn the card over, you'll see a line that says, 'For lost or stolen cards, call this number.'" And with that, she hung up!

"How can I turn the card over and call the number on the

back if I've *lost* the card?" I barked at the world in general (since the lady at the bank had abandoned me). Then I laughed—and there it was. The moment my pal Lynda had promised. When I'd called her that morning, pouring out my tale of woe about losing my credit card, she had said, "Oh, Barb, don't be upset. Maybe you'll find your card. And if you don't, I'll bet something will happen while you're looking for it that will make you laugh—and then you'll have another funny story to share with someone else who needs a laugh."

What a precious friend Lynda is! She knows just how to offer hope no matter what stressful situation I find myself in. She can say just the right words that send me off to search for something, believing that if I don't find it, I'll still come out ahead somehow. (Of course, the reason Lynda can have this attitude is that she's so scatterbrained she constantly loses things. It's part of everyday life for Lynda. She's lost so many things, the odds are overwhelming that while she's searching for the *newest* lost item she'll turn up something she lost last week—or last year. That's why she can be so hopeful as she tears her house apart.)

When you have a problem with something you've bought, it's nice to have a number you can call for help. Ideally, if your problem occurs during business hours, you can make that simple call, and a kind (and knowledgeable) stranger will provide the answer to your question.

When you have a problem with life, it's a special blessing to have a friend you can call and vent your feelings to, someone who knows you well enough to understand how you're feeling and who always manages to say just the right words that will give you hope. A friend who, just by listening and talking, has the ability to help you face your problem with a better attitude and stronger resolve.

And then there's the *real* source of *all* hope. How fortunate we are that we don't even need a telephone to reach him. There's no number to look up. He's always there, always alert, always listening, always helpful. So at any moment we can cry out to him, as the psalmist did: "Hasten, O God, to save me; O LORD, come quickly to help me" (70:1). And amazingly, we say "Amen" with a better attitude and stronger resolve because we've lost ourselves in him.

~ *Dear Father, thank you for my fellow sailors on life's seas—friends who give me hope and help. And thank you for being the ultimate Friend to me. Amen.*

Stained-Glass Redemption

NICOLE JOHNSON

~

Carry each other's burdens, and in this way you will
fulfill the law of Christ. (Galatians 6:2)

I had hired a truck to move my furniture from one part of the country to another. When it finally arrived I stood expectantly behind the vehicle as the door swung open. But something had gone terribly wrong. Inside the truck were all my possessions, but they were broken and damaged. The three-day journey had taken its toll on my furniture and belongings. I saw an antique rocking chair of my great-grandmother's with the arm broken in half, and it felt like my own arm was broken. I looked with dismay on a piece of marble that had gotten cracked and put my hand over my heart just to see if I could feel a crack in my heart. And when I saw a beloved piece of stained glass that was shattered, it was all I could do not to go to pieces. The loss was heartbreaking.

I turned away and cried. Many things I loved were broken. Things that couldn't be repaired. Things that could never be replaced. It was very hard to gather the pieces of furniture and glass and throw them in the trash. Several friends and family were with me and were as crushed as I was. One friend helped me gather the pieces of stained glass and took them away to dispose of them.

Along the road of life many of our most personal things get broken. Things that are important to us; things that have enormous value in our lives. And our hearts break with those losses. We feel fragmented, wounded, and shattered. Things that were once whole lie in pieces on the ground, and we aren't exactly sure what to do next. So we cry and grieve. Then, in time, we lean down and start to clean up the mess by picking up the pieces.

Sometimes we see another set or two of hands reaching for the broken chair or the shards of glass or the cracked marble. These hands are helping hands, healing hands. They hold us along with our broken dreams.

Last Christmas I received a present from my friend who had helped me pick up the pieces of the stained glass I had lost in the move. I opened the brightly wrapped box to discover one of the greatest gifts I've ever received. She had taken those pieces of broken glass and had them redesigned into a new piece of art. The stained glass was gorgeous. I was speechless.

As I sat holding her gift, she recounted to me the story of taking the pieces to throw away. She said she just couldn't let them go. At the time she wasn't sure what she would do with the pieces, but she wanted to see if there was any way to keep them. Then she found a craftswoman who saw the value and potential in the old glass and was thrilled with the opportunity to make something new from the pieces.

I stared at the piece of art in front of me. Nothing had

been wasted. All the pieces of broken glass had been put back in place. The brokenness made it so beautiful and interesting to me. It now hangs in front of a window where the light shines through it, showing off all the colors and shapes.

This is the most powerful picture of what we are to do with all the broken pieces of our lives. When we are shattered, wounded, and fragmented by life, we should never throw away the pieces. After we cry and grieve, we need to bend down and start to pick them up. Then, with other helping hands, we bring the pieces to God. And the Craftsman redeems them. He makes something new, beautiful, interesting, and whole. And his light shines through it, showing off all the colors and shapes of our brokenness.

～ Lord, forgive us for trying to throw away things that seem broken beyond repair. In your hands, nothing is unmendable. You redeem all things with the power of your love. You show us how good can come from the fragments and how your light can shine even more beautifully through the various cracks and colors of our brokenness. Show us how to pick up the pieces of our broken lives and the lives of others. May we be helping hands to one another as we trust in your redemptive work. Amen.

Throw Out the Lifeline

THELMA WELLS

*Also, if two lie down together, they will keep warm.
But how can one keep warm alone? Though one may
be overpowered, two can defend themselves. A cord of
three strands is not quickly broken. (Ecclesiastes 4:11–12)*

Do you ever feel like you're bobbing along in a life raft on life's seas while everyone else is safely aboard the luxury liner in the distance? Many women I've encountered at Women of Faith conferences and in my community feel like they are drifting and alone. They long for the camaraderie and security they perceive others are enjoying, but unless someone from the cruise ship throws them a lifeline, they feel like they might just drift away into oblivion. Many of these women are professionals, entrepreneurs, educators, specialists, and domestic engineers (stay-at-home moms). Many serve in some area of ministry. They are wives, mothers, community workers, volunteers, and students. All with similar cares and aspirations. And yet they feel alone and insecure, even insignificant.

Is there a voice that can call out to them, "You're going in the right direction. Keep on coming; you're doing good"? Is there a voice that can assure them, "I'm here to help you. Hold on! We're gonna get you out of that raft and on board with us"?

I can't count how many times I've heard women express a need for someone of maturity to say to them, "Hold on." "I'm here for you." "I'll help you." Women need mentors—other women who have sailed the seas of life a little longer and who will calm them, comfort them, communicate with them, be concerned about them, be committed to them, be compassionate toward them, be contagious with positive messages, and confront them with love.

That cry for community and connection resounded in my heart for several years until at last I decided to do something about it. I was reminded of Titus 2:3–5: "Older women likewise are to be reverent in their behavior, not malicious gossips, nor enslaved to much wine; teaching what is good, that they may encourage the young women to love their husbands, to love their children, to be sensible, pure, workers at home, kind, being subject to their own husbands, that the word of God may not be dishonored" (NASB). Realizing that I had a part of the lifeline women were crying out for in my hands, I drafted a course that I hoped would help them move from the insecurity of the raft into the comfort of the cruise ship.

It was an ambitious course that included goals and objectives like helping women get free from the effects of bias, prejudice, family issues, financial bondage, and other situations that rob them of their freedom to operate in the abundance of God. Through heart-to-heart encouragement and inspiration, I hoped to see women become empowered for greater service to the Lord.

The next step was to invite women to catch hold of the rope. I invited fifty ladies to my house for our initial meeting to see which ones were ready to come on board the ship. More than forty ladies came. Over the next nine months we worked together to get everybody safely on board. The course included discussions and homework, group projects, and a field trip to a Women of Faith conference. Rescuing women from their life rafts was frightening at times because we found that all of us had brought so much baggage on the trip that the whole ship was getting low in the water. So we had to throw some of it overboard.

We had baggage like abuse, depression, failing relationships, low self-esteem, financial insecurities, feelings of inadequacy, dysfunctional families, health issues, wayward children, lost dreams, unanswered questions, volatile emotions, lack of forgiveness, ministry hurts and disappointments, broken marriages, anemic spirituality, lack of purpose in life, pride and arrogance, and a whole lot more. You name the issue; we dealt with it using practical strategies and the Bible as our guide. There were some discussions that I, as the main facilitator, had little knowledge of, so there were many other mates who held on to the lifeline with me.

At the end of that first nine-month-long course, twenty-three ladies climbed from their flimsy rafts onto the cruise ship. Now many of these ladies are holding the lifeline in their hands, spotting other women in rafts and offering the same curriculum to them. Women who once felt alone and adrift are banding together on deck to offer hope and help to their mates still at sea.

I say, Girl, when you have a nudge in your spirit to do something, do it. You have the lifeline in your hands, just like I do. Throw out the lifeline and pull somebody off a flimsy raft onto the cruise ship of encouragement, inspiration, information, and empowerment. In the end, we can all enjoy the Captain's party together.

~ *Captain Jesus, you know when someone is about to flip over in her raft. You know when the seas are rough and the going gets tough. And you have chosen us as life preservers for the perishing. Help your daughters to notice the danger some of our sisters are in, and give us the desire and determination to throw out the lifeline. Thank you for the skill, knowledge, and stamina to hold tight until we have pulled everyone aboard. Amen.*

We're All Here

MARILYN MEBERG

~

But if we love each other, God lives in us,
and his love has been brought to full
expression through us. (1 John 4:12 NLT)

My good friend and doctor Christine Griswold took one look at the "odd thing" under Pat Wenger's left eye and said, "As soon as we finish here, I'm marching you immediately across the hall to see Dr. Blah-Blah" (not his real name).

"What for?" my dear friend Pat asked innocently.

"That growth under your eye looks bad to me."

Pat and I had dinner reservations at six. Since it was five o'clock, Pat felt the "thing under her eye" was not nearly the priority that dinner was. "I don't have time for this," Pat protested as Christine ushered her across the hall to see a plastic surgeon who specializes in "odd things" growing where they should not.

Dr. Blah-Blah took one look at the "thing" and announced mercilessly, "That's cancer . . . Why haven't you come in before this?" Faltering over his casual use of the word *cancer* and also feeling guilty that she hadn't tended to what looked like a pimple, Pat listened to the rest of the surgeon's comforting words. "I've seen hundreds of these kinds of cancer. We call them rodent cancers; it's as if a rodent were tunneling its way just under the skin, multiplying tissue and invading bone. Worst-case scenario is the loss of your eye." Mercy!

Pat was set up with a dermatologist who would cut out the cancer, and then Dr. Blah-Blah would take over to do the necessary plastic surgery. In his words, "We'll make every effort to eliminate as much disfigurement as possible."

Patsy Clairmont, Luci Swindoll, and I live a few blocks from Pat. We're a little community out here in the desert. We galvanized our energies into prayer support teams from all over our larger community of Women of Faith for the successful removal of all cancer and the preservation of Pat's eye.

On the morning of the great excavation, Patsy and I drove Pat to the doctor. Luci had a bronchial thing and we didn't want to risk it getting together with the rodent, so she stayed home to man the phones and be the commander of the Pat Wenger information center.

The procedure for the elimination of Pat's unwanted intruder was fascinating. It was explained that the dermatologist would cut out as much tissue as appeared to be cancerous. That tissue would be placed on a slide for immediate examination. Pat would come back to the waiting room with Patsy and me and wait for the report. If necessary, Pat would be called back for more cutting until the doctor was sure all the cancer had been removed.

After the first cut, during the wait, the three of us started playing "Quiddler." This is a word game that requires few brains but great creativity. It is necessary to convince the other players (and in this case some of the waiting room patients) that the word you've put together from your letter cards is a legitimate word. Pat was vociferously defending her word *boink* when she was called back for a second cut. There were more cancer cells.

Our spirits sank. We quickly affirmed *boink* as a great word and declared that she had won the game. (The only one who maintained she couldn't use *boink* was a crabby man who had so many skin cancers on his ears he was afraid he'd have to stop playing golf. His wife kept saying, "I've told you for years to wear a hat"—which didn't help his spirits. We felt he was entitled to be a bit crabby.)

I called the command center. "We need more prayer, Luci. Send out the word." Five hours later, after her fourth cut, Patsy and I were the only people left in the waiting room. Even the crabby man who should have worn a hat had gone. Pat finally came out with a huge bandage and an exhausted smile. "They got it all. I want a cheeseburger and fries."

The command center sent out the good report. We drove off for cheeseburgers and fries.

At 8:30 that night, Pat was "on the table" listening to Dr. Blah-Blah's exclamations over the depth and width of her incision. He turned out to be a master artist, however. With flesh "borrowed" from behind her ear, he filled the hole and sent her out the door shortly before midnight.

Les and Patsy Clairmont had been in the waiting room for hours in anticipation of driving Pat home. (I had a speaking engagement that night and hated not being available.) With nurturing gentleness they saw her into her house and into bed. Wonderful friends . . . fabulous neighbors.

The next day Luci brought Marie Callender's vegetable soup, corn bread, and pie to Pat's for lunch. Our little desert community sat around the table laughing, eating, and reliving portions of Pat's experience.

Pat looked horrible that day. Whenever I felt overwhelmed and on the verge of tears, I kept saying, "You don't have cancer, baby; you don't have cancer." What Pat does have is a gang of people who would not leave her side during that storm. All available hands were on deck loving her as God loves her. We were all there; so was he.

∼ *Lord, what a source of hope you enable us to be when we find our loved ones in a storm. Thank you for your example of how to put love into action. Amen.*

Together, Forever

SHEILA WALSH

*Let us consider how we may spur one another
on toward love and good deeds. Let us not give up
meeting together, as some are in the habit of doing,
but let us encourage one another—and all the more
as you see the Day approaching.* (Hebrews 10:24–25)

One of the greatest gifts in my life is being part of the Women of Faith team. I am not a huge fan of travel, and we travel about thirty weekends every year; but what I look forward to every time is seeing those familiar faces in the lobby of the hotel when we arrive. I watch my son's face light up as he spots Mary Graham or runs to show Luci Swindoll some new bad habit he's acquired at school, sure she will approve. I see my husband, Barry, hug Marilyn Meberg, and I know how much her friendship means to him.

The highlight of each weekend for me, however, is Friday evening before the conference starts. We gather together for a couple of hours—speakers, musicians, and worship team. We eat and sing and pray. It's a sacred time for all of us. It's a safe place where we can unburden ourselves from the cares of the week, share our concerns, and be loved and encouraged. It's a time when we can express our frustration with ourselves or bring physical needs to friends who will handle our hearts and our tears with grace and mercy.

We have stood together at the funerals of Barry's parents. We have gathered around Luci's hospital bed when she was undergoing tests for an irregular heartbeat. We have sat together in the waiting room for hours as Barbara Johnson was in surgery for a brain tumor. We have celebrated New Year's Eve together and numerous birthdays. We have taken vacations together or stayed over in a city just to be together for another day. We have laughed our way through countless photo and video shoots and commiserated with the poor makeup artist as she attempts to get us to keep our mouths shut long enough for her to apply lipstick.

We are very different. Patsy is a human dynamo onstage, but offstage she is quiet and thoughtful and loves to read and share a new thought or idea. Thelma is caring and sweet, always ready with a song or a scripture to encourage us. Marilyn is crazy—in the best possible way! She is hilarious and brilliant and one of the best listeners you could ever find. Luci is a darling, full of funny stories and great ideas of ways to celebrate the simplest moment. Nicole is witty and cosmopolitan, kind and tenderhearted. Barbara, when she traveled with us, was always watching out for everyone else, making sure we were okay, and teaching my son, Christian, silly little songs or new places to stick his bubble gum. Now she does it over the phone!

We are very different. What we have in common is a passionate love for Christ, for truth, and for grace—and a deep commitment to our friendship.

It seems to me that one of the ills of our culture is a sense of alienation, of being disconnected and adrift. We were made for community, and when we live in isolation we carry our burdens alone. The writer to the Hebrews recognized our tendency to pull away from one another as life becomes more complicated and days are dark. His words speak to one of our deepest needs today: "Let us not give up meeting together, . . . but let us encourage one another—and all the more as you see the Day approaching" (10:25).

Those words are a call for "all hands on deck." We each need to find a place where we can throw in our heart and soul with others who love God. We need to receive the fragrance of Christ that we bring when we gather in his name. Friends can lift our heads when our shoulders are sinking and stand with us through tears and laughter. How thankful I am for my sisters and brothers in Christ, intended by God to be together, forever.

~ *Father, thank you for my fellow believers. Thank you for those who love you and stand with me. Help me to be faithful and committed in the precious relationships you have given me. Amen.*

PART SIX

~

Land Ho!

"Are We There Yet?"

PATSY CLAIRMONT

If I take the wings of the dawn, if I dwell in the remotest part of the sea, even there Thy hand will lead me, and Thy right hand will lay hold of me. (Psalm 139:9–10 NASB)

My thing is arrivals. Departures are fine, but I want to get where I'm going—now. Impatient? Uh-huh. And excited. Slowly I am learning that half the joy of arriving is in the planning and the journey. Yet, for me, the greatest kick in a venture is spotting my destination. Land ho!

When I was a child, I went on vacations with my family, and before my dad could even pull out of the driveway, I was stretched out in the backseat on a makeshift feather bed draped across the floorboard (no seat belts in those days). I buried my head inside a stack of comic books (*Little Lulu, Archie,* and *Huey, Duey, and Louie*—great literary mind I had) until I read myself asleep. I did this so I could shorten the transit and get right to the arrival. My mom would try coaxing me, "Patsy, you're missing everything staying down there. Look at the mountains, trees, lakes, people, and houses." But the only times I surfaced were to smell the gasoline (Is that legal?) as Dad pumped our tank full and to fill my tank with hamburgers, milk shakes, and potato chips (a true connoisseur).

What would I have done if I had been in Moses' caravan? Yikes! Forty years of reading *Beetle Bailey* between the humps of a camel? Nah, it wouldn't have worked. Besides, camels spit. Yuck. They may be the ships of the desert, but let one glob of fluid from their loose lips land on me and I'd be sinking that craft.

If I had left Egypt when I was a kid and didn't arrive in the Promised Land until I was middle-aged, imagine how many times, with my hurry-up personality, I would have said, "Are we there yet?" I'm sure Moses would have relegated me to the back of the sandal parade to bleat with the sheep and therefore miss the first "Land ho!" sighting.

Promised Land—what a handle of hope. Perhaps that is why spotting our destination buoys our spirits. We think each new location may contain all that we've been waiting for, hoping for, and dreaming of—a land flowing with milk and honey.

The Israelites didn't leave Egypt and instantly arrive in Canaan. In fact, the Lord sent them the scenic route. Scenic? Oh, I know it was the barren wilderness, but think of what they saw and heard along the way—the parting of the Red Sea, manna falling like rain, rock-gushing streams, victories against troubling factions, fire by night, the thunderous voice of God, and so on. They witnessed the miraculous. Who would have wanted to miss that?

Actually, even with all my attempts to arrive speedily, it has been the things I've seen, heard, and experienced along my life journey that have been faith producing. Why, it was in the wilderness years, when I was an agoraphobic, that I witnessed the Lord's deliverance up close and personal. During those years I was aware of his hand parting my fears, of his nurturing provision for my shriveled soul, of his refreshment for my parched existence, of his direction for my wayward feet, and of his voice counseling my confused heart. It was quite literally miraculous, and as long and as hard as those years were, I would not have wanted to miss what I experienced of God.

~ *Jehovah God, how gracious of you to follow us down into the valley, up onto the precipice, through raging rivers, and across the desert floor. How divinely comforting to know that we cannot wander outside of your jurisdiction, that we cannot experience need beyond your ability to provide, and that you, a holy God, are on speaking terms with us. Help us not to be so focused on our plans that we miss your way or so distracted that we are unaware of the miraculous. Thank you for the promise that one blessed day we will arrive (Land ho!) in Glory, the forever land of milk and honey, where sin will no longer distort us or sully our view of you. Amen.*

Obnoxious or Persistent?

THELMA WELLS

~

Let us hold unswervingly to the hope we profess, for he who promised is faithful. (Hebrews 10:23)

A funny thing happened to me on the way to my banking career. My husband and I banked at this particular bank for over ten years. I was already working at another bank on a part-time, working mother's program. One day after updating my résumé, I called One More Time Bank in Texas and spoke to the personnel manager. I informed him that I wanted to bring my résumé to him in about ten minutes. I lived close to the bank. He informed me that the bank was about to close and I could bring it another day.

"No, I'm going to bring it now. Please meet me in the lobby of the bank and I'll give it to you," I said.

Without success he tried to convince me to bring it another day, but I was determined. When I met him in the lobby, he immediately informed me that there were no openings. "That's fine," I replied. "You will have some and you'll call me." (I had a lot of gall, girl!)

Two weeks passed without a word from One More Time Bank. I called and talked to the same gentleman I had met in the lobby. He told me the same thing: "We have no openings at this time." I waited another week before calling back, then another week, and another. When I called for the fourth week and was given the same one-liner, I responded, "That's just fine. I know you will have an opening and you will call me in for an interview. I'll be patient. Thank you."

In a few days I got the call I had been waiting for. Little did I know that this was only a ploy to keep me from calling again! The personnel manager had me interview with somebody who had no idea how to interview a person. She asked things like, "If we hire you, you do know you are going to have to wait on white people, don't you?" I didn't make myself look any brighter when I answered with something like, "Naw, you don't mean it—help white people? Hello! That's all that comes in here anyway." I left knowing nothing was going to come of that interview.

I was right. Another two weeks of silence passed. That's when I reinstated the ritual of calling every week. After about a month I received a call to come for another interview. They were serious then. The lady I spoke with was charming, intelligent, and ready for business. In less than three days I had a job offer from the personnel manager.

"Mrs. Wells, this is Mr. Banker calling to offer you a job as a new accounts clerk. Your starting salary is $400 per month."

"Thank you, Mr. Banker, but $400 is not enough for me to get out of my bed to come to work. I must have more."

"Mrs. Wells, this is where we start all new employees."

"Well, that's not going to work for me. But you'll call me back. I'll look forward to hearing from you soon. Bye-bye."

In about fifteen minutes I got the second call.

"Mrs. Wells, this is Mr. Banker again. We can offer you $450 per month. Will you come?"

"No, sir, I will not. I appreciate the offer. But I have a college degree and working experience, and I'm not a slow learner. You need me and I need you. Call me back when you can pay me for coming. Talk with you later."

I waited a long hour for the phone to ring again. It finally did.

"Mrs. Wells [he sounded irritated], this is Mr. Banker again, and I just talked to the president of the bank. He said to offer you $500 per month and not a penny more."

I said, "Thank you very much, Mr. Banker. When would you like me to start?"

The negotiations ended and my banking career began the following Wednesday.

Perhaps I was a little obnoxious. Or maybe just persistent. However you measure it, I had confidence that this was where God was sending me to work, and nothing and nobody would deter me from the hope he'd placed in my heart. I was not worried or discouraged with the lengthy process. I had put value on my ability to do a superior job for them if they hired me. The energy of expectancy motivated me to stand firm in what may have looked to some people like a no-win situation. I saw it only as a challenge to be conquered. Three years later I became a banking officer. The personnel director hugged me and told me what an asset I was to that bank.

Your immediate hope may not be in a job or negotiating for money. But whatever you're hoping for, if it is helpful to you or someone else, if your goals and vision are pure, if you are sure God is directing you, be persistent. Never give up. Follow through. Keep paddling straight ahead until you reach the dock.

～ *Sweet Jesus, when you give us a clear direction to follow, you also give us the grit and gall to go full steam ahead. You have plans for our lives, and you give us all what we need to reach our destination. Grant us the spiritual discernment to know the difference between your plan for us and our plan for ourselves. When we follow your plan, we know that all things will work out for our good. Amen.*

Safely in Hope's Camp

LUCI SWINDOLL

*Hope deferred makes the heart sick, but a longing
fulfilled is a tree of life. (Proverbs 13:12)*

There's a powerful segment in the 1994 movie *The
Shawshank Redemption,* in which Andy Dufresne (por-
trayed by the actor Tim Robbins) defies authority and plays a
small portion of a Mozart opera, *The Marriage of Figaro.* It's
the famous "Letter Duet" from the third act, which will make
your heart swoon, it's so beautiful. I've heard that opera many
times myself and I know its beauty well. Locking himself in an
office, Andy puts the music on the P.A. system, and it wafts
across the airwaves through the walls of Shawshank prison for
everybody to hear.

The effect is mesmerizing. No one could have imagined a
group of hard-core prisoners would be moved by something so
foreign to their experience, but they were spellbound until the
music ended. Of course, this was more than a major infraction
of the rules; it was grounds for solitary confinement according
to the very strict, overbearing, unconscionable warden. And,
as you know if you saw the movie, Andy is indeed thrown in
the "hole" for two weeks for that little stunt.

The next scene takes place in the prison mess hall, where Andy, unshaven and disheveled, joins his friends for the first time at the table. They question him about whether being in the hole was worth playing that music. Unwaveringly, he assures them it was. He says, "We need it so we don't forget."

"What are you talkin' about?" probes "Red" Redding (played by Morgan Freeman).

"Hope. That there are places in the world that aren't made out of stone," Andy says. "That there's somethin' inside that they can't get to, that they can't touch. It's yours."

Red, who has already served more than a quarter century of his life sentence for murder, answers, "Let me tell you something, my friend. Hope is a dangerous thing. Hope can drive a man insane. It's got no use on the inside. Better get used to that idea."

Hope is dangerous only when you believe in it. When the odds are against you but you don't give up; when you're hopelessly at the end of your rope and you hang on anyway; when you can't go any lower then begin to look up—these are the times you find hope and everything changes. "Exiles feed on hope," wrote the ancient Greek playwright Aeschylus. It's daily bread to them. It becomes the very cell structure inside that keeps them alive.

That was true of the apostle Paul when he was held captive in prison. He never gave up hope, and some of his most brilliant, encouraging letters were written while he was behind bars. In Hebrews, the author refers to hope as "an unbreakable spiritual lifeline, reaching past all appearances right to the very presence of God" (Hebrews 6:19 MSG). When we're secure in that kind of hope, watch out, world! We're dangerous. We're not willing to "get used to the idea" that our soul will remain in chains. Nothing can keep us down.

Hope is irrepressible. But unless that hope is founded in Christ, it's just wishful thinking. Apart from him, there's no way to be set free from what binds us. The price of real freedom is paid when one believes Jesus has the keys to the prison door, asks him to unlock it, and then walks out into the sunlight.

Catherine Marshall wrote about the difference between acceptance and resignation. Resignation gives up and settles down, but acceptance opens its hands to what a loving Father sends. "Acceptance never slams the door on hope," Marshall says.

When a dear friend of mine was told she had stomach cancer, she never gave up her hope in the goodness and presence of God. As her body began to deteriorate and the cancer moved into her liver, she never gave up hope. As she became bedridden and could barely speak, she never gave up hope. There was no question this disease was going to take her life, but she doggedly and dangerously dared to fight the good fight of faith to the very last breath. She was not willing to defer hope for a better day, and when she died in March of 1995, the object of her hope was realized—she met her Savior face to face. Even as her body weakened, her soul was being held secure by hope, the lifeline of her faith.

Regardless of what happens today, or tomorrow, or next year, hope is alive. Life is fragile and our days full of uncertainties. Nonetheless, God has given us hope. Look for that cell structure inside yourself and find the hope God has placed there. Let it flourish. Don't resign yourself to a world carved out of gray stone.

Andy Dufresne left a letter for his friend Red to find when Red was finally released from prison after forty years. "Remember, Red. Hope is a good thing, maybe the best of things, and no good thing ever dies. I will be hoping that this letter finds you, and finds you well. Your friend, Andy."

If a prisoner in an apparently hopeless situation can hold on to hope, then we who trust in a faithful God to give us all the hope we'll ever need are already safely in hope's camp. Our fulfilled longings have become a tree of life on the shore of solid ground.

~ *Faithful Father, hope is an unbreakable spiritual lifeline between me and you. I receive it as my own and hang on to it for dear life, trusting you will provide all I need for whatever I will face. Amen.*

Waiting for the Light

BARBARA JOHNSON

~

*My soul waits for the Lord more than watchmen
wait for the morning. (Psalm 130:6)*

In Newgrange, Ireland, there is an ancient, mysterious structure called a passage tomb. A friend who described his visit there painted such a fascinating picture that it stayed in my thoughts for days. Although the tomb was built more than three thousand years before Jesus came to earth—and so could *not* have been built by Christians—it provides a striking illustration of how Jesus' coming brought hope to our lives.

On the outside, the tomb is a large, rounded mound of earth surrounded by carved stones. Inside, a passage about twenty yards long leads to what is assumed to be a burial chamber. The most amazing thing about the tomb is what happens there at sunrise on five mornings during the year.

To the people of ancient Ireland, the seasons changed as the arc of the sun's daily passage overhead moved higher or lower across the sky. As summer waned and the days grew colder, the sun's path shrank away to the south. The ancient ones did not know why this happened, so it must have been frightening for them. They knew the sun had always come back in the past, but they probably worried that a time would come when the sun would move away, taking summer's warmth with it, and keep on going forever. So they watched eagerly for signs that the sun was on its way back again. Ironically, one of the places they watched was inside the passage tomb in Newgrange.

The time when the sun reaches its farthest distance from the Northern Hemisphere and begins its turn back is called the winter solstice. That was the event the ancient people of Ireland watched for. They wanted to reassure themselves that the sun was coming back again to turn their fields green and make their crops flourish. Somehow they calculated this phenomenon so precisely that they were able to build structures that could catch the sun's first rays of light specifically on those mornings as it turned back to the north. The tomb at Newgrange is one of those places. Inside the tomb, for only a few minutes at sunrise during the winter solstice, a shaft of sunlight passes through an opening in the mound to shine directly down the tomb's passage and illuminate the burial chamber.

Imagine the ancient ones gathered there during the cold December nights, waiting. Imagine how long the night must have seemed to them as they watched for the sun's rays. They had no clocks to tell what time it was. They could only wait and watch nervously for the light to come.

Hearing my friend tell the story, I thought of all the long nights I've spent waiting. Waiting to hear a teenage boy come in from a date late at night. Waiting in train stations and airports. Waiting in hospital hallways. Waiting for the phone to ring. Waiting eleven years for a wayward son to come home . . .

Remembering the times and places where I've waited, I

think of those people so long ago who waited anxiously in the ancient tomb's dark passage. To them, everything depended on a single beam of sunlight they hoped would suddenly shine into their darkness. If the light didn't come, they knew they were doomed. But all they could do was sit in the tomb and wait.

How different that is from the way Christians wait today. Jesus promised he would come again, and we know he will. We don't have to worry he will turn away from us and keep on going. Because of the hope he shared with us, we can wait, even in places of fear and darkness, with courage and fortitude. Because we know that, whatever the immediate outcome, our long-term future is secured.

We pray for rescue from whatever threatens us. We pray that suffering will be eased, that challenges will be overcome, that lives will be spared. Yet we know that even if God's answer is not the answer we asked for, everything will be all right in the end. Hope is the unbreakable spiritual lifeline that will hold us securely through every earthly danger until one day we're pulled from the storms of life and deposited on the shores of our heavenly home. In every earthly difficulty, we are there in the passageway of the tomb with those early ones, anxiously watching and waiting for the light to shine and take away the darkness. The difference is the hope we have in God's promises.

If the sun doesn't come up tomorrow, we won't despair. We'll be dancing in the streets of heaven with him.

~ *Dear Jesus, your love lights up the dark places of our lives. We watch for your return with hope and longing, eager to spend eternity with you. Amen.*

Hobbling Home

SHEILA WALSH

~

*A bruised reed he will not break, and a smoldering
wick he will not snuff out. In faithfulness he will bring
forth justice; he will not falter or be discouraged till
he establishes justice on earth. (Isaiah 42:3–4)*

I used to think of myself as someone who didn't exercise regularly, but I realize now that can't be true, as I fly into the Dallas airport on a regular basis. Anyone who arrives in Dallas and has to catch a connecting flight faces an Olympian challenge.

One day I arrived at gate 2 in terminal A and my next flight left out of gate 43 in terminal C. My carry-on bags were heavier than usual, as I was doing research for a new book and had several study guides and commentaries in my briefcase. I looked to see how close I was to the underground rail transport and was delighted that I was only two gates away. As I approached the entrance, an official-looking woman with a very assertive smile stopped me.

"It's out of order today," she said, grinning from ear to ear.

"I'm not sure you should smile when you tell people that," I suggested. "It's misleading."

"Have a good day!" she insisted.

I walked over to the airport map muttering under my breath. It would have been impossible to walk any farther than I was going to have to walk that day. I had an hour before my flight, so I set off at a determined pace.

If we have met, you will know that I like to wear heels. I don't wear them because I think they make me look better or taller; I actually like them. When I wear flat shoes I feel like a duck, so most days I view the world from at least a three-inch advantage. That day I had on my purple suede boots. I dumped my bags on the floor of one of the moving walkways and stared out the window as black clouds began to fill the sky and large drops of rain pelted the tarmac. I prayed that my flight would not be canceled. I was tired and I just wanted to get home.

"Watch out!"

I turned to see who was yelling at me and promptly fell off the walkway.

"I was trying to warn you that it was coming to an end," an apologetic man said as he helped me up.

"Thanks!" I said with a weak smile. I tried to walk on and thought, *I don't remember having this limp this morning.*

I looked down and the heel of my right boot was gone, snapped clean off. I picked up the books that had scattered all over the place and tried to march forward with my left foot in a healthy boot and walk on my tiptoes with my defective right one. I looked totally ridiculous, like a drunken Long John Silver. After a few steps my calf hurt so badly that I reverted to hobbling, up and down, up and down. I caught sight of myself in the glass window of a store that I was limping past and started to laugh. I laughed so hard I had to put my bags down and hold on to the back of a chair.

My cell phone rang. It was my husband. I could hardly talk.

"Are you all right?" he asked.

"I'm great! I have two more miles to walk, it's starting to storm, and the heel broke off my boot," I spluttered.

"That does sound like fun," he said, not quite getting it.

There are days on our journey when all we can do is hobble, totter, and stagger along toward home . . . and that's okay. Because God will never falter, or even be discouraged, until he accomplishes all he has planned for us and his kingdom. We have a firm promise from God that even when it seems as if more than our heel is broken, he will watch over us. It may seem sometimes like we are close to a breaking point; but our hope is in a faithful God who says that although we may be bruised, we will not be broken. We may feel some days as if our light is dim and the storm gathering just outside our window threatens to extinguish it, but God promises that we will not be snuffed out.

So let's just keep our chins up and keep on hobbling.

⌣ *Father, some days are dark and difficult. Help us to remember that even on those days you are with us and you give us the grace to hobble. Amen.*

Something to Crow About

PATSY CLAIRMONT

O LORD, our Lord, how majestic is your name in all the earth!
You have set your glory above the heavens. (Psalm 8:1)

A crow's-nest (different than, say, crow's-feet, which are indelibly hovering on my eyescape) is a high-above-the-seas perch for sailors to view distant ships. Actually, I'm not a big fan of crows; they seem a tad aggressive, even sarcastic—although I wouldn't mind catching a view from their "nest" to gain their vantage point.

I have loved birds in general since childhood, which was when I heard the first strains of "Somewhere over the Rainbow." Remember that oldie? That's where bluebirds fly, and to this day bluebirds remain my favorite winged creatures. But I also like doves. Their peaceful coos are like love-whispers, which when you consider their generous size seems a fairly restrained sound. Imagine scratchy squawks emanating from those puffy birds; why, they could cause quite a neighborhood ruckus.

Recently a pair of doves chose our rooftop to perch on and selected the eaves at our side entry to nest under. Being bird-friendly, I thought their arrival sweet, except every time we entered or exited our home the pair got their attitudes in a wad. The doves would fly out overhead in a great flurry of feathers, sounding like sheets flapping in a windstorm. For some reason, this always caught me by surprise even though it happened every day. The frantic fluttering of two birds in a dither every time we stepped out our door increased all of our heartbeats.

I do like the fact, though, that doves are seldom alone. They are either in a pool of company dining on sidewalk crumbs, dotting the statues (and I do mean dotting) in parks, or paired up for . . . well, nesting purposes (it would be a shame to let all that lovey-dovey talk go to waste).

My full-bodied winged friends are also freckled—and I'm crazy about freckles whether sprinkled liberally across a youngster's face or speckled over a dove's countenance. Freckles make me smile. And so did the doves when they weren't ruffling my feathers with their hasty departures.

Doves are mentioned more than once in Scripture. They're harbingers of hope. Take, for instance, the dove that was released from Noah's ark. The first time he sent out a dove it returned in short order because there was no place for it to perch, which signaled that the waters were still covering the earth. The second time it returned with an olive leaf in its beak, which meant things were improving. A week later the dove did not return because the waters had subsided and the dove was in line at the unemployment office. Okay, so you may need to read it for yourself (see Genesis 8:8–13), but the point is, the dove gained a reputation as a gentle bearer of good news.

A dove is also mentioned in the romance between the Shulammite bride and her lover. Listen in . . .

> How beautiful you are, my darling,
> How beautiful you are!
> Your eyes are like doves.
>
> (Song of Solomon 1:15 NASB)

Aww. I wonder if that's when we coined the word *"lovebirds."*

Speaking of lovebirds, last week upon my return from a conference, I found some sweet talk awaiting me from my bridegroom of forty-one years. See what you think:

> My love for you is always there,
> Even though I have no hair!

Doesn't seem to have the same tender sentiment as Solomon's, but, hey, it has heart . . . uh, I mean hair . . . oh, never mind.

Another scriptural dove sighting is in the lament of David during trying times when he cried, "Oh, that I had wings like a dove! I would fly away and be at rest" (Psalm 55:6 NASB).

Last week when I drew back my curtains, I saw something that caught my attention. It was a circle of white, like snow on the grass. But I was in the desert, and even without a crow's-nest to scan the horizon, I knew that with the thermometer registering seventy degrees, snow wasn't a possibility. So I stepped out onto my patio for a closer look. It was dove feathers, at least a hundred of them scattered willy-nilly. I dashed to the side entrance and there was no fluttering of wings and no sign of my honeymooners. There also were no body parts, no blood (whew), and no forwarding address.

I'm not certain if the lovebirds read David's plea and flew the coop to be at rest, but I know this for certain: One glorious day I'll be out of here as well. Whether by natural causes or by supernatural intervention, this ol' bird is going over the rainbow where bluebirds fly. So if you come upon my circle of feathers, don't fret. I'll be circling the throne worshiping at the feet of the one who causes us to mount up and fly.

~ *Lord, sometimes I need the crow's-nest perspective. I need a higher view, lest I forget that this life is temporary and it's heaven that is eternal. Just writing those words causes my soul to coo and my spirit to rise up and long to soar. Thank you for hope, the glory-wind beneath my wings. Amen.*

Fact or Fantasy?

MARILYN MEBERG

~

The eternal God is your refuge, and his everlasting
arms are under you. (Deuteronomy 33:27 NLT)

I love the story of an elderly couple who enjoyed having
younger couples over for dinner. They liked to bridge the
generation gap and usually had fun in the process. During one
of those dinners, a young husband noted how gracious and
loving the old man was to his wife, calling her "Doll Face,"
"Darling," "Honey," and "Pumpkin."

While "Pumpkin" was in the kitchen getting coffee, the
young man said, "I'm impressed with your love for your wife.
I think it's wonderful that after all these years you call her
those loving pet names."

"I have to tell you the truth," the old man responded.
"About ten years ago I forgot her name."

Perhaps one of the reasons that joke gives me a giggle is my
increasing inability to remember names. I'm not talking about
people I barely know or to whom I've just been introduced. I'm
talking about people I've known for years. I can't tell you how
many times I've frantically rifled through my mental file in an
effort to retrieve a name I should know, only to realize the file

is empty. I'm greatly comforted, however, because I remember the details of any personal story I'm told. "Oh, yeah, I remember her. She was munching cheese and crackers during her husband's funeral service. Now what was her name?"

Is there any hope for me in the realm of name retrieval? No . . . I'm getting worse rather than better. Do I wish there were a possible "file fill-up" for me? Of course. But wishing is not the same thing as hoping. Wishing has no reality base; it is instead an indulging in fantasy. Hope, on the other hand, contains a realistic expectation of fulfillment. I know better than to indulge in fantasy. Reality says I will experience an increase in "Pumpkins" along my path.

Children can charm us with their fantasy vision, but it is because they are children and not adults that we find ourselves charmed. For example, my five-year-old grandson, Alec, and I were chatting on the phone yesterday. Without a segue into the subject, he abruptly announced he was going to be baptized. Since he had been resistant to the idea, Beth (his mother) wisely told him to tell her when he was ready. Apparently he'd decided he was ready.

I commended him on his decision and asked what had changed his thinking. He went into a long diatribe about hating the taste of the water in the church drinking fountain and that if he were baptized he could have Communion. I was quiet a moment as I tried to trace his logic. He became impatient with me and said, "Maungya . . . you can't have Communion unless you're baptized, and I want juice instead of that water in the fountain. Not only that, Maungya, bread comes with it."

Alec hates it if anyone laughs at what he says, but I couldn't control myself. I went into gales of laughter. There was a long-distance pause and then a click. He had hung up and huffed away.

When Beth called me back, she developed Alec's baptism logic further. Apparently during the last church Communion service, Alec had asked Ian for a sip of his "juice." When Ian refused, Alec tried to bargain for Ian's bread. That didn't work either. Obviously Alec had no choice but baptism if he wanted his very own snack.

When Pat Wenger's three-year-old grandson, Derek, was visiting from Tennessee last spring, I offered to take him for a ride in my convertible. He didn't seem to enjoy it; in fact, he was eager to go back to Grandma's. Later Derek told Pat he felt really, really sorry for me. When she pressed him about his feelings, he said it made him sad I was so poor; I had only enough money to buy half a car. He wanted to give me some of his birthday money so I could go and buy the other half. Sweet baby!

If I told you those two anecdotes came from adults, you would not be charmed; you'd be alarmed. We make allowance for children who are constantly working their way to an understanding of what is real in life and what is not.

The much-loved Mr. Rogers of the famed children's television program *Mr. Rogers' Neighborhood* did a tremendous service to his little viewers when his song "Wishes Don't Make Things Come True" was featured. He repeatedly discussed the meaning of the song and taught that wishing didn't make fear go away or pain disappear. Perhaps we all need a dose of Mr.

Rogers as we occasionally lapse into childish expectations and wishful thinking.

It was Jesus who invited the children to come to him, the source of all hope, comfort, and strength. It was and continues to be Jesus who calms our fears and eases our pain. At any age we have the hope and assurance of God's "everlasting arms" under us as well as around us. That fact is as real as my inability to remember your name.

~ *Lord God, may I always remember that you are my refuge. Because my hope is in you, I am held in your arms forever. Amen.*

This Is the Hope

SHEILA WALSH

*I pray also that the eyes of your heart may be enlightened
in order that you may know the hope to which he has
called you, the riches of his glorious inheritance in the
saints, and his incomparably great power for us
who believe. (Ephesians 1:18–19)*

Someone wrote that God made people because he loves stories. That is obviously a simple statement, but it is true that we each have our own story. The tapestry of my life has been enriched by those who have entrusted me with some of their stories even as they have received some of mine.

I will never forget a woman I met at one of our conferences in the Midwest. She and her mother had purchased tickets to attend the conference together, and then the mom was diagnosed with a particularly virulent type of cancer. By the time of the conference, her mother had died. The daughter came alone.

"My mom was pretty lucid up until the end," she told me. "She had her Bible in bed with her and would love to read verses to me that she thought would encourage me. But it was in the last week before she died that she said something that puzzled me," she continued. "She kept saying, 'That's the hope!' She said it over and over. I would ask her what she meant, but she just smiled and slipped off to sleep again. After she died I was taking the linens off her bed and there was her Bible under the pillow. There was a bookmark in it and a passage underlined: 'I pray also that the eyes of your heart may be enlightened in order that you may know the hope to which he has called you, the riches of his glorious inheritance in the saints, and his incomparably great power for us who believe' [Ephesians 1:18–19].

"I knew then what she meant when she kept saying, 'That's the hope!' My mom has been in love with Jesus since she was a child, but to see the joy and peace she experienced even in her pain when her time was almost over is something that has changed me forever."

It is a privilege to be granted the opportunity to be a witness as a follower of Christ crosses the river. Not all crossings are as peaceful as the one shared with me that night in Chicago. Sometimes there is pain or confusion, which is distressing to observe. At times the person is gone in a moment and we are left with a feeling of unfinished business or unshared words. There can be a reluctance to leave, a resistance to the new and unfamiliar song of eternity.

What we can rest in, however, is that no matter what the crossing is like, we have the absolute assurance of the riches of his glorious inheritance in the saints. Paul's prayer was that the "eyes of our hearts" would be opened, that there would be an inner awareness—a God-given understanding of the hope we have in Christ at all times. That hope is the assurance of eternal life to come, guaranteed by the present possession of the Holy Spirit who lives in us at this moment, always calling us on toward our eternal home. When we are finally able to cry out, "Land ho!" more than we could ever dare to imagine becomes the story of our new lives. This is the hope.

One of my favorite hymns is "Guide Me, O Thou Great Jehovah." It was written by William Williams, a Welshman, in the eighteenth century. It was sung in Welsh in the 1941 Academy Award–winning movie *How Green Was My Valley.* It was sung in English in 1997 at the funeral of Diana, Princess of Wales. The words are a cry of faith to the one who is a pillar of cloud by day and a pillar of fire through the darkest night.

If days seem dark or uncertain, raise your voice with thousands who have gone before you and sing out your hope!

> Guide me, O Thou great Jehovah,
> Pilgrim through this barren land;
> I am weak, but Thou art mighty;
> Hold me with Thy pow'rful hand;
> Bread of heaven,
> Bread of heaven,
> Feed me till I want no more,
> Feed me till I want no more.
>
> Open now the crystal fountain,
> whence the healing stream doth flow;
> Let the fire and cloudy pillar
> Lead me all my journey through;
> Strong Deliverer, strong Deliverer,
> Be Thou still my strength and shield;
> Be Thou still my strength and shield.

When I tread the verge of Jordan,
Bid my anxious fears subside;
Bear me thro' the swelling current,
Land me safe on Canaan's side;
Songs of praises, songs of praises
I will ever give to Thee,
I will ever give to Thee.

It's a "Land ho!" promise.

～ *Father, thank you for the promise I have in you for all eternity. May I rest in your faithfulness this day. Amen.*

Keep Your Hopes Up!

THELMA WELLS

~

*May the God of hope fill you with all joy and peace as
you trust in him, so that you may overflow with hope
by the power of the Holy Spirit. (Romans 15:13)*

The Pacific Ocean was a foamy azure blue that day
about noon. The smell of the ocean filled our nostrils.
Sea gulls spotted us watching them and performed their landing routines with birdlike precision. Small motorboats lined
the docks, skimming back and forth on the water in harmony
with the waves. The noonday sun beamed down upon us, and
the temperature was a perfect seventy degrees. Just right for
basking and meditating on the goodness and awesomeness of
God.

Suddenly crowds of people began to invade the peacefulness
of the moment that my friend and assistant, Pat, and I were
enjoying. Lines formed to board the resting boats and hook up
to parasailing equipment. I knew those boats were not waiting
on me, because I don't parasail. But I got the surprise of a lifetime when I jokingly turned to Pat and asked her if she wanted
to try her skill. I was only kidding. Didn't she know that?

Miss Pat informed me that she was indeed thinking about

going up. It was something she had always wanted to do. "I just want to see what it's like to be that close to heaven," she said. My reply was, "Go ahead with yo' bad self. I'll be in the boat waiting for you to land. You'll never find *me* over that much water holding a little thin rope or line or whatever they call it. I'll take your picture while you take your life into your own hands."

We paid our fare and boarded the motorboat. The captain gave us instructions. I'm glad Pat heard them. I was too busy trying to put film in my camera so I could take a picture of the brave lady who was going out to sea, tied to a little seat, holding on to a rope. Lord, have mercy!

My greatest fear was that water would splash in the boat and I would get my hair wet. (That's always my greatest caution around water.) The motor started. Pat was strapped in, either concentrating on her instructions or giving herself last rites. My camera was ready. And off we went.

Soon, Pat started lifting off, and up, up, up, she went. Was it a bird? Was it a kite? No, it was Patricia! My little camcorder was moving and weaving with the current, but I had a great view of Pat's face high, high in the sky. She was smiling, praying, singing, and obviously having the time of her life. I actually felt happy for her. Her hope had been fulfilled.

Pat landed back in the boat without even getting her hair wet. "I saw a bird's-eye view of what God sees every day," she reported. "I saw the island of Honolulu, but I could just imagine what he sees all over the universe! My initial thought was, *How great Thou art!* Then I started singing it. My last thought coming in for the landing was, *Thank you, Jesus! Please, just don't let a whale jump up.*" (It was whale season.)

Jesus came that we might have life—and life abundantly more than the ordinary, sometimes mundane routines we experience. There's nothing wrong with those, but sometimes we get an opportunity to experience that adventure that's been tucked in the back of our minds, ever since we were children.

Often my granddaughter, Vanessa, lies down on her bed with her hands clasped and eyes staring into space. When I ask her what she's doing, she says, "Oh, just thinking."

"What are you thinking about?" I ask.

"Just thinking about taking art classes, because I'm good in art."

"You sure are good in art, and one day you are going to take those art classes you're thinking about," I assure her.

"Yeah, I know. I hope it's soon."

I plan to make this little girl's hopes and dreams come true because I love her so much.

Just think about how much God loves us, his little girls! God never has to ask us what we're thinking about. He knows our hopes and desires, our aspirations and dreams. He loves us much more than I can ever love Vanessa, and I love her with all my heart. Just as I want to make Vanessa's dreams come true, God wants to make ours come true. That's what he did for Pat on that sunny day in Hawaii.

I've heard it said, "Don't get your hopes up." My question is, If you don't get them up, where are they going? After Pat experienced the grandeur of the near-heavenly atmosphere, I believe her heart was saying, "My body may be coming in for the landing, but my spirit is staying high in the sky."

Moments of hope fulfilled will come your way many times

in life. Be ready to get strapped into the seat, hold on to the rope, be lifted high in the sky, and let your spirit soar. Keep your hopes up!

~ *Overseer of the universe, we praise you for the experiences of abundance in life that you plan for us, just because you love us so much. Every little fleeting dream catches your attention, and at the right time you surprise us with fulfillment. Thank you. Remind us to keep an open mind and be ready to seize the moment when you lavish your love on us. Amen.*

There's No Place Like Hope

NICOLE JOHNSON

*For in this hope we were saved. But hope
that is seen is no hope at all. Who hopes for
what he already has? (Romans 8:24)*

She clicked her ruby slippers three times, and each time she said, "There's no place like home." It was where she wanted to be more than anywhere else in the world. Home was the place that made everything make sense for Dorothy. She was from Kansas, and she was trying to survive in the Land of Oz. She had suddenly awakened in a world with munchkins and scarecrows and wicked witches, and home was the place she wanted to get back to.

We, too, find ourselves in a world we can't understand. We are Dorothys in a world that rarely feels completely safe to us. We hunger to get to a place that feels like home, a safe place where things are good and familiar and warm. We grow tired of the strangeness and harshness of the world we see when we look around us. We long for a place we can be surrounded by love and care, friends, and lots of "Auntie Ems."

That place is hope.

For it is hope that helps us make sense of this world in which we are living. It is hope that says, *What you see with your eyes is not all there is. Look closer and you will see there is so much more.* And as we start to see the bigger picture, our hope grows. We can make more sense of the suffering and troubles around us. We can see signs that there is real and deep meaning in this world, and that sparks our hope.

Unfortunately, hope has no strength of its own. We can't hope in hope; we have to put our hope in something else. So the strength of hope lies in what it hopes *in*. That means that what we put our hope in really matters. If we put our hope in lesser things, we set ourselves up for disappointment. If we hope that we'll get a promotion and our boss favors someone else, we're crushed. But if we put our hope in God's provision for our lives, promotion or not, our hope grows as we see God work, because we've put our hope in something strong enough to sustain us.

And a mere promotion isn't nearly strong enough. We can hope for a promotion and get it, only to realize that what we were really hoping for was not a fatter wallet, but a richer life. And a promotion alone can't provide that.

Our hopes have a unique way of guiding us to what our hearts truly hunger for. And this is our real hope: that there is order behind the universe and that things make sense no matter which way they go. When we feel out of control and lost, we hope desperately that someone is in control. But only God can stoke the fire of hope with that kind of assurance, because he is the one in control. And as he reassures us that he is looking after us, we can put more and more of our trust in him.

Trust is hope with gray hair. A little older, a little wiser, still waiting, still anticipating, still hoping—but believing at the same time. Believing in the order and the good even when it can't always be seen. Trust is the older sister of hope who lives with quiet confidence, standing tall in a world that she doesn't always understand. She teaches us to close our eyes and click our ruby slippers and whisper, "There's no place like hope. There's no place like hope. There's no place like hope."

~ *Lord, you are not the Wizard of Oz; you are the God of the universe, the only one who can truly show us how to get home. We've lost the yellow brick road, but we trust that you are the Way and that you are guiding our every step. We place our hope in you and ask you to mature it into deep and profound trust, today and every day. Amen.*

CONCLUSION

Safe Harbor

PATSY CLAIRMONT

❧

As I sit to pen my reflections on safe harbors, America is teetering on the brink of war. The news reports say we are hours away from bombing, and people in the Middle East are hunkering down in the safest places they can find. We in the States are concerned for the welfare of our soldiers. We also ache for the innocent families in Iraq who suffer the peril brought on them by their treacherous leader.

Since the devastating events of September 11, 2001, Americans also wonder more consciously and routinely about how our "homeland security" will be affected as we face potential threats. We are unsure of our safety from Al Qaeda, sleeper cells, and lone wolves. We are living in uncertain times.

But we don't have to have the threat of war or terrorist attacks hanging over us to know we are in a battle. In the past months I have talked to a number of friends and acquaintances, and without exception they reported staggering difficulties in their lives: life-threatening illnesses, financial reversals, radical teenage rebellion, heart-wrenching divorce, unemployment, war deployment, and so on. When these hardships hit like crashing waves, they can take our breath away if not infringe upon our faith. We cry out, "Lord, where are you?" We need a safe harbor!

We are most likely to experience a sense of safety when we feel secure, provided for, and well protected. And we are offered that in Christ—just not in the way we had imagined. For while Christ offers us refuge, he doesn't guarantee exemption from pain, loss, or heartbreak. Naturally, that is what we'd like: a risk-free, painless existence. Yet anyone who has lived long enough to attend, oh, say, preschool, has figured out that life is testy. In fact, I believe life is one tough curriculum.

During my twenties I was emotionally and physically housebound because of a condition known as agoraphobia. I loved the Lord but decided he must not be too fond of me, because even though I was in the safety of my own home, I was drowning in a tidal wave of fear.

More than thirty years have passed since those years when it was all I could do to keep my head above water to take my next breath. Yesterday I wrote a psalm about my struggle:

> I was tossed about in the raging storms of my anxiety,
> The waves of fear encompassed me.
> The strength in my body melted,
> The sounds of death filled my head.
> Angry winds splintered my vessel,
> I clung on in desperation.
> I cried to the Lord and he heard me.
> He heard me over the lashing storm,
> Through my wailing fears, in my utter weakness,
> And above my warring thoughts.

He heard me, and the waters stilled as I grew quiet, and
I entered the safety of his harbor.

Here's what I learned in my attempts to reach the harbor:
When Jesus rescues us, often it is not by removing us from the
storm but by reassuring us in the midst of the storm. You see,
Jesus is our harbor. We don't have to reach land to experience
what that means. Jesus is our safety. We don't have to be out of
harm's way to be immersed in his care. Jesus is our protection—
get this—even when the winds continue to howl, our ship continues to list, and solid land is nowhere in sight.

This means we can be confident that a soldier, even in the
throes of combat, can experience the peace that passes all
understanding. Those going through the deep waters of grief
can know divine consolation. Those whose jobs are threatened
can experience new levels of God's provision. And when any
of us is emotionally in over our head, we can know the power
of his right hand to save and to steady.

Sheila, Thelma, Barbara, Marilyn, Nicole, Luci, and I have
learned that we don't have to try to row across the ocean of our
lives alone, because he who walks on water is the Captain of
our vessel and the Harbor for our souls. And that realization
has brought us hope . . . irrepressible hope.

ABOUT THE AUTHORS

Patsy Clairmont is an acclaimed speaker whose presentations have thrilled audiences in venues ranging from churches to the Pentagon. She is the author of more than a dozen titles, including *God Uses Cracked Pots*. Her latest book, *I Grew Up Little,* is her autobiography, a story of hope.

Barbara Johnson's outreach, Spatula Ministries, and her many best-selling books, including *Humor Me, Plant a Geranium in Your Cranium,* and *Living Somewhere Between Estrogen and Death,* have helped millions of hurting people learn to laugh again.

Nicole Johnson is a gifted writer and dramatist whose powerful vignettes about life and an ever-faithful God have touched millions of hearts at Women of Faith conferences. The host of *Mid-Point* on the Hallmark channel, Nicole's latest book is *Keeping a Princess Heart in a Not-So-Fairy-Tale World*.

Marilyn Meberg has enjoyed a lifetime of careers aimed at helping others: as an instructor at Biola University for ten years, then as a professional therapist, and now as a laughter-loving Women of Faith speaker and author. Her most recent best-selling book is *The Decision of a Lifetime*.

World traveler **Luci Swindoll** celebrates life wherever she goes. A former oil company executive and vice president of Insight for Living, she was a pioneer in the contemporary Christian women's book market with titles including *You Bring the Confetti, God Brings the Joy.* Her latest book is *I Married Adventure.*

Sheila Walsh uses words—sung, written, and spoken—to bring hope to millions. Born in Scotland, Sheila became a U.S. citizen in 2003. Her latest releases are *The Best of Sheila Walsh,* a collection of inspirational Celtic music, and the book *The Heartache No One Sees.*

Thelma Wells is president of A Woman of God Ministries in Dallas and travels globally teaching others to overcome barriers. She holds a master's degree in pastoral ministry and mentors women in the U.S., India, and Africa. Her book *Girl! Have I Got Good News for You* is used as a Christian college curriculum.

EXTRAORDINARY*faith*

CONFERENCE *2005*

2005 EVENT CITIES & SP ECIAL GUESTS

NATIONAL
CONFERENCE
LAS VEGAS, NV
FEBRUARY 17-19
Thomas & Mack Center

NATIONAL
CONFERENCE
FT. LAUDERDALE, FL
FEBRUARY 24-26
Office Depot Center

SHREVEPORT, LA
APRIL 1-2
CenturyTel Center
Sandi Patty,
Chonda Pierce,
Jennifer Rothschild

HOUSTON, TX
APRIL 8-9
Toyota Center
Kristin Chenoweth,
Natalie Grant,
Jennifer Rothschild

COLUMBUS, OH
APRIL 15-16
Nationwide Arena
Avalon,
Kristin Chenoweth,
Nichole Nordeman

BILLINGS, MT
MAY 13-14
MetraPark
Sandi Patty,
Chonda Pierce,
Jennifer Rothschild

PITTSBURGH, PA
MAY 20-21
Mellon Arena
Natalie Grant,
Nichole Nordeman,
Chonda Pierce

KANSAS CITY, MO
JUNE 3-4
Kemper Arena
Natalie Grant,
Chonda Pierce,
Jennifer Rothschild

ST. LOUIS, MO
JUNE 17-18
Savvis Center
Avalon,
Nichole Nordeman,
Chonda Pierce

CANADA &
NEW ENGLAND
CRUISE
JUNE 25 – JULY 2
Tammy Trent

ATLANTA, GA
JULY 8-9
Philips Arena
Natalie Grant,
Sherri Shepherd,
Tammy Trent

FT. WAYNE, IN
JULY 15-16
Allen County War
Memorial Coliseum
Sandi Patty,
Chonda Pierce,
Jennifer Rothschild

DETROIT, MI
JULY 22-23
Palace of Auburn Hills
Sherri Shepherd,
Tammy Trent,
CeCe Winans

WASHINGTON, DC
JULY 29-30
MCI Center
Natalie Grant,
Nichole Nordeman,
Sherri Shepherd

SACRAMENTO, CA
AUGUST 5-6
ARCO Arena
Avalon,
Kristin Chenoweth,
Tammy Trent

PORTLAND, OR
AUGUST 12-13
Rose Garden Arena
Kristin Chenoweth,
Natalie Grant,
Tammy Trent

DENVER, CO
AUGUST 19-20
Pepsi Center
Avalon,
Kristin Chenoweth,
Nichole Nordeman

DALLAS, TX
AUGUST 26-27
American Airlines Center
Avalon,
Kristin Chenoweth,
Nichole Nordeman

ANAHEIM, CA
SEPTEMBER 9-10
Arrowhead Pond
Avalon, Chonda Pierce,
Tammy Trent

PHILADELPHIA, PA
SEPTEMBER 16-17
Wachovia Center
Kathie Lee Gifford,
Natalie Grant,
Nichole Nordeman

ALBANY, NY
SEPTEMBER 23-24
Pepsi Arena
Sandi Patty,
Chonda Pierce

HARTFORD, CT
SEPT. 30 – OCT. 1
Hartford Civic Center
Sandi Patty,
Chonda Pierce,
Tammy Trent

SEATTLE, WA
OCTOBER 7-8
Key Arena
Sandi Patty,
Chonda Pierce,
Jennifer Rothschild

DES MOINES, IA
OCTOBER 14-15
Wells Fargo Arena
Sandi Patty,
Chonda Pierce,
Jennifer Rothschild

ST. PAUL, MN
OCTOBER 21-22
Xcel Energy Center
Sandi Patty,
Chonda Pierce,
Jennifer Rothschild

CHARLOTTE, NC
OCTOBER 28-29
Charlotte Coliseum
Sandi Patty, Beth Moore,
Sherri Shepherd

OKLAHOMA CITY, OK
NOVEMBER 4-5
Ford Center
Kristin Chenoweth,
Sandi Patty,
Chonda Pierce

ORLANDO, FL
NOVEMBER 11-12
TD Waterhouse Centre
Avalon,
Chonda Pierce,
Tammy Trent

1-888-49-FAITH womenoffaith.com

Guests subject to change. Not all guests appear in every city. Visit womenoffaith.com for details on special guests, registration deadlines and pricing.

Interested in books by Patrick Morley?
A Patrick Morley Reading Guide

Want a Success That Really Matters?

Want to Reinvent Yourself?

Personal Reflections

For Men in Transition

Man in the Mirror Workbook

Practical Direction

A Compelling Evangelism Tool

Want a Deeper
Walk with God?

Practical Theology

Devotional

For You

Want a Stronger
Family?

For Her

For Both
of You

Solving the 24
Problems Men Face

THE MAN IN
THE MIRROR

PATRICK M. MORLEY

For Son

Are you a leader interested in reaching and discipling men in your church and community?
Man in the Mirror can help!

FREE **Call 888-MIRROR1 and ask for your free copy of *Ten Practical Secrets to Attract and Retain Men.*** These ideas are already working in churches all across America.

MAN
—IN THE—
MIRROR
Serving Church Leaders who Reach Men

www.maninthemirror.org
* Books for $1 *
* Leadership Training *
* Dynamic Local Church Events *
* Bible Studies for Men *
* New Book – *The Dad in the Mirror* *